The Human Capital Playbook

The Human Capital Playbook

Strategies for Leaders to Hire, Inspire, and Retain Talent

ANGELA TAIT

The Human Capital Playbook: Strategies for Leaders to Hire, Inspire, and Retain Talent

For more information, email **talent@taitconsultingllc.com**.

ISBN: 979-8-89694-060-9 - eBook

ISBN: 979-8-89694-061-6 - Paperback

ISBN: 979-8-89694-062-3 - Hardcover

Get Your Free Gift!

Use my free job description template to attract the right talent! Download it from my website and start creating strategic job descriptions that truly work.

You can get a copy by visiting:

https://bit.ly/freejobdescription.

This book is dedicated to my husband, Ryan, for his unwavering support and guidance; my children, Henry and Oliver, who I hope will one day follow this path as business owners; and my parents, who taught me the values of work ethic, relationships, and a growth mindset.

And to all the companies and clients who gave me the opportunity to work and grow alongside them—this book is dedicated to the leaders who relentlessly pursue meaningful impact within their teams and organizations. Your commitment to investing in people and building a people-first culture rooted in growth, empathy, and excellence transforms workplaces into communities that empower and inspire, where employees invest back into the business and its vision.

Foreword

Angela Tait has proven she has what it takes to empower growth-minded small businesses to increase engagement, improve retention, and buy back their time (as my friend Dan Martell might say) by hiring top performers, coaching leaders, and building employee development systems to gain more profitability.

She is recognized all over the world as a premier HR and talent management leader and has helped companies of all sizes exceed their growth goals. She's got the credentials to back all of this up by earning her Master of Science in Organization Development at Pepperdine University.

In *The Human Capital Playbook,* Angela astutely shares the most effective ways for leaders to hire, inspire, train, and retain talented people. I love how she's laid it out in three practical parts:

1. HIRE

2. INSPIRE

3. RETAIN

In each part, Angela focuses on sharing stories of how she and others have succeeded (and failed) in various ways, and she gives you the tools to do the same within your business. My favorite books are packed with fascinating stories, empirical evidence (the science that makes the stories true), and practical application (the "So what, why should I care? How can I actually implement this stuff?"). Angela does that in spades in this book.

What sets this work apart is its focus on human capital as both a science and an art. Through a blend of research, case studies, and practical frameworks, it offers tools that not only optimize performance but also foster a culture of innovation and inclusion. The author masterfully addresses the challenges leaders face today, from managing diverse teams to navigating the complexities of the digital age.

As someone who has witnessed firsthand the transformative power of effective talent management, I can confidently say this book will inspire and empower you to lead with clarity and compassion. Whether you're a seasoned leader or new to the field, it offers wisdom and strategies that will benefit your organization and the individuals within it.

I urge you to read this book, take notes, and, most importantly, *take action* from what you learn. It could change your life ... if you'll let it.

—Ryan Hawk, Host of *The Learning Leader Show*

Author of *Welcome to Management, The Pursuit of Excellence, The Score That Matters*

Table of Contents

Part 2: Inspire

Part 3: Retain

Chapter 7 Effective Onboarding and Integration 110

Chapter 8 Continuous Employee Development and Career Pathing 127

Introduction

"When given the proper tools and the trust to be empowered and make decisions, HR can be one of the most vital voices at the table."

—S<small>TEVE</small> W<small>YNN</small>

W hy is Human Resources essential for a company, especially a small business? A CEO once joked, "Why do I need HR when I only have ten people?" Fast forward to his 100th hire, and he admitted, "HR was vital for our business success!"

HR isn't just about filling seats—it's about building culture, driving productivity, and fostering growth. According to Workhuman, a people-first culture can boost productivity by an average of $1,737 per employee annually.[1] Despite this, many misunderstand

---

1   Workhuman Editorial Team, "How to Create a People First Culture in 2024 + What It Means," Workhuman, September 5, 2024, https://www.workhuman.com/blog/people-first-culture/.

HR's role, equating it with policies and paperwork rather than its true function: empowering people and accelerating business success.

Dave Ulrich, known as the "Father of Modern HR," mentions in his book *HR from the Outside In: Six Competencies for the Future of Human Resources* that "HR professionals are storytellers, strategy interpreters, and facilitators of change. They guide organizations through external challenges, nurture internal growth, and equip teams to thrive. They are learners, teachers, and emotional caregivers—essential to any thriving business."[2]

A strategic HR function offers companies significant advantages, including:

- **Attracting and Retaining Top Talent**: Drawing in exceptional individuals and keeping them engaged.

- **Building a Strong Company Culture**: Creating an environment where employees feel valued and supported.

- **Managing Performance**: Helping teams set and achieve goals through feedback and development.

---

2   David Ulrich, *HR from the Outside in: Six Competencies for the Future of Human Resources* (New York: McGraw-Hill, 2012).

- **Ensuring Compliance and Reducing Risk**: Safeguarding businesses by adhering to regulations and mitigating legal exposure.

- **Fostering Leadership and Growth**: Equipping employees with the skills to excel personally and professionally.

Whether you're a startup or an established enterprise, HR is a strategic partner that fuels growth and sustains success. Are you ready to put people first?

THE STRATEGIC HEARTBEAT OF BUSINESS GROWTH

HR plays a multifaceted role in a company's success, going far beyond managing employee files or handling paperwork. Think of HR as the engine driving growth by aligning the right people with the right opportunities.

At the heart of HR's impact is talent acquisition, where strategic sourcing ensures the company attracts individuals whose skills and values align with its mission. Organizational growth depends on having the right talent in place, and HR creates a pipeline of innovative, driven employees.

Equally important is employee development. Through targeted training and professional programs, HR enhances skills, prepares employees for future leadership roles, and sustains long-term success. HR also mediates workplace conflicts, turning challenges into opportunities for collaboration and growth, and ensures legal compliance to protect the company while aligning performance with organizational goals.

Employee engagement and well-being are directly tied to success. HR cultivates a culture where people feel valued and motivated, designing compensation, benefits, and succession plans that retain talent and ensure business continuity. Data-driven insights further shape workforce strategies, enhancing performance and driving profitability.

Yet, in many small businesses, HR functions are often fragmented and managed by office managers or assistants who may lack specialized skills. This can lead to costly hiring mismatches or unclear job descriptions. That's where investing in a skilled HR partner becomes invaluable.

Whether it's an HR Business Partner (HRBP), fractional HR support, or a VP of People, a qualified HR professional does more than fill roles—they align talent with strategic goals, foster employee development, and drive retention by creating a healthy, inclusive environment. By laying the foundation for long-term success, HR's holistic approach saves money, increases productivity, and fuels growth.

FINDING MY PATH: BUILDING HR FROM THE GROUND UP

When I joined a real estate development company in Phoenix, AZ, in January 2020, I stepped into a tight-knit team of ten. It felt like being the new kid at school—everyone seemed to know each other well, leaving me feeling like an outsider. Coming from a non-traditional HR background, I felt the pressure to prove myself to the leadership team. Despite often being labeled as underqualified or overqualified in previous job searches, I was determined to make a meaningful impact.

Before transitioning into HR, I spent nearly a decade excelling in sales—a field that sharpened my resilience, negotiation skills, and adaptability but never fully ignited my passion. Pivoting in my late twenties, I earned a master's degree in organization development from Pepperdine, gaining global experience on real-world business challenges. Yet, breaking into HR without traditional credentials wasn't easy. After a brief return to sales, I launched a virtual coaching business, where I facilitated leadership development masterclasses and collaborated on HR projects, strengthening my skills and network.

The turning point came when I landed an executive recruiter role with a large firm. One conversation about a controller position unexpectedly led to an offer for an internal Human Resource Business

Partner (HRBP) role. They needed someone to build an HR department from scratch—a daunting challenge for someone without conventional experience. But I embraced the opportunity, channeling my non-traditional background into creative solutions.

On day one, I stepped into chaos. The company was preparing for a major acquisition, growing from ten to thirty-five employees almost overnight. I had to create onboarding processes, implement benefits, and navigate a new HRIS system—all while managing the challenges of a global pandemic. That first year, as the sole HR professional, we hired over 100 people. It was messy, high-pressure, and deeply rewarding.

These experiences reshaped my approach to HR. I learned to look beyond polished resumes, hiring for passion and potential instead. I also realized that HR is not just about filling roles but creating a culture where people can thrive. There were moments of immense fulfillment—watching employees grow, fostering inclusion, and making a positive impact in challenging times. But the relentless pace, combined with being a new mom, also left me grappling with burnout.

As I reflect on this journey, one lesson stands out: success in HR and business begins with investing in people. The following pages will guide you through this process, from recruiting top performers to building a people-first culture. Together, we'll explore strategies for hiring not just for today's needs but also for long-term growth and innovation.

OVERVIEW OF PART 1:
HIRE (FOCUS: RECRUITMENT AND SELECTION)

- **Chapter 1: Crafting Clear Roles (The Key to Effective Hiring)**

  - **Role Clarity:** This chapter sets the foundation by outlining the importance of well-defined roles in the hiring process. It emphasizes how clear job descriptions and expectations not only attract qualified candidates but also enhance overall team alignment. Key components include breaking down role responsibilities, required competencies, and measurable outcomes. This clarity aids in setting the right expectations from the start, leading to better hiring decisions.

- **Chapter 2: Building a Winning Team (Attracting and Selecting Talent)**

  - **Talent Attraction:** This chapter explores strategies for attracting top talent by creating compelling job postings and leveraging employer branding. It delves into the role of effective sourcing, social media presence, and candidate engagement in building a winning team. The chapter highlights the significance of aligning candidate values with the company's mission and culture, creating a mutual sense of purpose and commitment.

- **Chapter 3: Mastering the Interview Process**

  o **Interview Excellence:** This chapter focuses on the interview process as a critical step in hiring success. It covers everything from preparing for interviews to structuring questions that reveal a candidate's skills, values, and cultural fit. It includes techniques like the STAR method and different types of interview questions (behavioral, competency, and values-based). The emphasis is on creating a consistent, bias-aware, and effective interview process that ensures both parties have clarity and confidence in the hiring decision.

Part 1: "HIRE" sets the stage for a strategic approach to building an exceptional team from the ground up. Hiring isn't just about filling a role; it's about envisioning the potential impact of the right individual on your organization's future. By defining roles clearly, aligning your company's values with candidate expectations, and mastering the interview process, you create a foundation that attracts and retains top talent. Each chapter in this section will guide you through essential steps, from crafting compelling job descriptions to structuring interviews that reveal a candidate's true fit. Let's start with Chapter 1, where we lay the groundwork for success by defining roles with clarity and purpose.

PART 1

Hire

Focus: Recruitment and Selection

"One machine can do the work of fifty ordinary men. No machine can do the work of one extraordinary man."

—ELBERT HUBBARD

Almost fifteen years ago, I went skydiving near Sydney, Australia. It was an experience of pure exhilaration—the rush of freedom falling through the sky, mixed with moments of sheer terror about what could go wrong. This balance between risk and reward perfectly mirrors the challenges I often encounter in life and business.

Opportunities and new experiences bring excitement, but doubt can creep in, making us question our next steps. Just like during that skydive, when I clung tightly to my guide—my parachute, my safety net—there are times when we hold back, hesitant to embrace the opportunity to take the leap.

In business, this feeling is widespread when hiring. For many, bringing on new talent can feel as thrilling yet daunting as jumping out of a plane. But if we let fear hold us back, we risk missing the immense potential the right team can unlock.

That's why I'm passionate about helping business owners confidently approach hiring. I've been through it countless times, understanding the challenges and rewards of making the right hiring decisions.

Hiring is more than filling a position—it is discovering an extraordinary individual who can elevate your organization. This requires a strategic, intentional approach. It begins with a clear, well-crafted job description that defines your expectations, the skills needed, and the qualities of your ideal candidate. It's more than a list of duties; it's a blueprint communicating your vision and goals.

However, attracting extraordinary talent goes beyond the job description. It's about showing potential hires what sets your company apart—opportunities for growth, a culture of flexibility, meaningful relationships, and a people-first environment. When candidates can see a future with you, they're drawn to your organization.

Finally, hiring isn't complete without a thoughtful interview process. This crucial step helps you identify not only a candidate's skills but also their alignment with your company's needs and aspirations. By asking the right questions and listening closely, you can find the person who will be a catalyst for growth and innovation.

As we move into Chapter 1, "Crafting Clear Roles: The Key to Effective Hiring," we'll explore how to build job descriptions that attract top talent, align with your company's mission, and lay the foundation for a successful hiring process. Let's begin the journey of hiring with intention, clarity, and a focus on long-term growth.

Chapter 1

Crafting Clear Roles: The Key to Effective Hiring

*"Always hire people who
are better than you."*

—SHERYL SANDBERG

When a legal client handed me a job description for a critical role, it was clear why their search for top talent was falling flat. The description, a single, vague paragraph, barely scratched the surface of what they needed. It lacked clarity, direction, and any sense of what the company truly valued in its next hire. Without a well-crafted job description, finding the right candidate is like searching for a needle in a haystack. So, I took it upon myself to transform that bare-bones paragraph into a strategic blueprint by breaking it down into five key parts.

1. **Company Overview and Purpose**: This section provides a cohesive introduction that highlights the company's mission, values, and culture, as well as the role's objectives. This allows candidates to understand the company's vision and how the role contributes to its goals, aligning expectations from the outset. Well-crafted overviews attract candidates who not only meet qualifications but also resonate with the company's ethos, increasing the likelihood of finding a strong cultural fit.

2. **Job Title**: The job title should be clear, specific, and reflective of the role's responsibilities. It should accurately describe the level of the position and its primary function, helping candidates quickly understand the role's scope. A precise title not only attracts the right applicants but also sets internal expectations for the position, ensuring alignment across teams.

3. **Duties/Responsibilities**: This section outlines the primary tasks the job entails, specifying daily, weekly, or monthly duties. Clear, detailed responsibilities help candidates self-assess their fit for the role and understand exactly what will be expected of them. It also minimizes misunderstandings during the hiring process and beyond, contributing to greater employee satisfaction and retention.

4. **Required/Preferred Qualifications**: This section specifies the necessary skills, experience, education, and qualifications a candidate must have to be considered for the role. Including preferred qualifications gives potential candidates an understanding of what could set them apart. Being clear about qualifications not only ensures better candidate matches but also streamlines the selection process, saving time for both the recruiter and hiring manager.

5. **Compensation and Benefits**: Here, you list the salary range, benefits, and perks associated with the role, such as health insurance, retirement plans, and vacation time. Including this information upfront signals transparency, which can improve candidate engagement and trust. It also helps potential hires evaluate the total package, increasing the likelihood of attracting individuals who are genuinely interested and a good fit.

Including these five key parts in a job description helps create a comprehensive, appealing overview that attracts qualified candidates, sets clear expectations, and ultimately reduces turnover. Society of Human Resource Management (SHRM) research shows well-defined job descriptions can reduce hiring time by 12 to 15 percent. A strong job description not only fills positions faster but also contributes to better overall team cohesion and improved performance outcomes.

REAL-LIFE SUCCESS

One of my clients struggled to find qualified candidates for a key position. After revising their job description using this five-part approach, they noticed a 50 percent increase in qualified applicants. They also filled the position within thirty days, compared to the previous search that had dragged on for months. A LinkedIn study found that 72 percent of hiring managers agree that clear job descriptions are crucial for attracting the right candidates.

AVOID THESE COMMON PITFALLS

It's also important to avoid common mistakes, such as using too much jargon, being overly broad, or omitting crucial details. These errors can deter the right candidates or attract unqualified applicants, prolonging the hiring process. Statistics show that well-crafted job descriptions are like magnets for top talent. According to Indeed, clear job descriptions get 36 percent more applications than vague ones.

TIPS FOR JOB DESCRIPTIONS
AND HIRING SUCCESS

- **Make It Descriptive Yet Concise**: Provide clear details about the role's responsibilities, required skills, and expectations, but avoid excessive jargon and overly long lists. Highlight what's essential to keep it impactful.

- **Use Clear, Inclusive Language**: Avoid gendered language or phrases that might alienate potential candidates. Instead, utilize inclusive language that appeals to a diverse talent pool, promoting equity and openness.

- **Highlight Growth and Opportunities**: If the role offers opportunities for advancement, mention this briefly. Candidates are drawn to positions where they can envision future growth.

- **Showcase Company Culture and Values**: Briefly describe the company's mission, vision, and values. This attracts candidates who resonate with your company's ethos, creating a foundation for long-term alignment.

- **Be Transparent About Benefits and Flexibility**: Include any unique benefits, work-from-home options, or flexible hours. These details can make a significant difference in attracting candidates who prioritize work-life balance.

This approach ensures that each job description is comprehensive yet inviting, clearly defining roles and responsibilities. An effective job description sets the tone for accountability and performance, positioning both the candidate and the company for long-term success. When the company isn't a household name, a well-crafted job description is a powerful first impression that attracts candidates aligned with the company's vision.

SMALL ADJUSTMENTS

A few months ago, I posted a job on LinkedIn that garnered around eighty views but didn't receive a single application—a clear sign that something was off. I revised the job description, tweaked the title, and narrowed the salary range to better align with the market and the role's requirements. These small adjustments made a significant difference; I quickly saw more applicants who were a good fit. This experience also taught me that different job boards cater to different types of roles, making it essential to diversify where you post jobs. By using multiple platforms and actively sourcing candidates who meet your qualifications, you can increase your chances of finding the right hire.

There can be many reasons someone isn't applying for a position, so it's essential to refine and pivot your job postings continuously. The goal is to increase the number of applications to build a broader pool of candidates, which ultimately helps identify the best fit for the role. With more candidates to choose from, it becomes easier to compare qualifications, experience, salary expectations, and education levels.

ESSENTIAL TOOLS AND STEPS

Today, AI-powered tools offer tremendous support in crafting effective job descriptions. Platforms like Indeed and LinkedIn provide suggested bullet points from similar roles, helping to enhance your job description with language that resonates with potential candidates. These tools can significantly improve the visibility and attractiveness of your postings.

In one instance, a business owner handed me a job description for a role he needed to fill. When I asked how he created the bullet points, he admitted to copying and pasting from various similar roles he found online. This approach can be effective, as it allows you to customize the description to fit the specific needs of the position. However, I noticed he hadn't cross-checked the description with the person currently in the role, even though that individual was leaving voluntarily. I suggested he review the list with the outgoing employee to ensure accuracy and relevance, making any necessary adjustments. This step is crucial for setting clear expectations and ensuring that the next hire is set up for success from day one.

Another useful strategy is to have the person currently in the role track their daily tasks for a week. This provides a clearer understanding of the role's responsibilities and highlights areas that may need additional training for the new hire. If possible, encourage the outgoing employee to create templates or standard operating procedures (SOP), including resources and tools, to make the transition smoother for the new hire coming on board to fill the position. This might not always be possible, depending on the situation. Still, in cases where the employee has been given a specific notice period, it's an invaluable opportunity to capture their knowledge and experience before they walk out the door.

As businesses grow, they often need to hire multiple people for newly created roles to meet expanding demands. In these situations, it's crucial to collaborate with key stakeholders, including the hiring manager, to identify what skills, attributes, and resources the new hires will need to be successful. This approach helps establish clear expectations during the interview process, reducing the risk of misalignment later. Ensuring that candidates are well-suited for the role not only sets them up for success but also helps get the position off the ground smoothly.

This is especially vital when the role is brand new and will require the hired individual to establish structure as they onboard. Since these roles often evolve beyond the initial scope, it's important to be transparent during interviews, emphasizing that this is a new position. Setting this tone from the start ensures candidates understand that there may be ambiguity and less structure initially. It also helps identify individuals who are adaptable and comfortable in navigating change.

However, while transparency is key, it's equally important to provide as much structure and consistency as possible once someone is hired. Regular check-ins, clear communication, and gradual role definition foster better alignment and job satisfaction. The more clarity you can provide early on—both about the evolving nature of the role and the support available—the more likely you are to find someone who thrives in the position and contributes to the company's growth.

A good rule of thumb is to create a job description for every position within the company. This provides both the employee and the manager with a benchmark of the key elements of the role, and it's also useful for employees who aspire to move up in the company. Job descriptions can serve as a reference during performance reviews to assess whether someone is fulfilling their responsibilities effectively before considering a promotion. At a previous company, we created job descriptions for every role and had each employee review their own to ensure accuracy, adding or removing responsibilities as needed. These job descriptions then became valuable tools in the hiring process for future replacements, as they accurately outlined the role's responsibilities and requirements.

ROLE CLARITY: THE FOUNDATION OF SUCCESS

At the company I worked for, I encountered a situation where an employee believed she was excelling in her position and even expected a promotion. However, her manager had a very different perspective—he was considering firing her due to what he saw as poor performance. The disconnect was startling. I suggested a one-on-one conversation using the job description as a guide to clearly outline the responsibilities, priorities, and metrics for success in the role. This meeting provided much-needed clarity, and as a result, the employee became more engaged and productive, now understanding exactly what was expected of her. This experience underscores the importance of role clarity and continuous communication between employees and management. When employees know exactly what's required of them, they're better positioned to meet or exceed those expectations, contributing more meaningfully to the organization and finding greater motivation in their work.

Role clarity goes beyond simply outlining tasks; it involves creating a framework that supports ongoing growth and improvement. New employees often come in eager to make a positive impact, but their success is heavily influenced by the clarity and structure they encounter. In my pre-screens, when I ask candidates about their ideal work environment, the most common responses include a desire for support, clear communication, and working cohesively towards a common goal. These elements are integral to creating a workplace where employees can thrive.

According to McKinsey research, achieving true role clarity is closely linked to overall organizational performance and health.[3] Establishing this clarity should begin by defining roles before considering the people who will fill them. The focus should be on identifying where the greatest potential value lies within the role, along with the skills and behaviors necessary to unlock that value. This approach allows companies to set clear expectations and define success from the outset, ensuring that teams are better aligned and capable of driving strong outcomes.

In Verne Harnish's book *Scaling Up*, a chapter on hiring introduces a tool called the "Job Scoreboard."[4] This tool is particularly useful for enhancing role

3   Mike Barriere, Miriam Owens, and Sarah Pobereskin, "Linking Talent to Value," McKinsey & Company, April 12, 2018, https://www.mckinsey.com/capabilities/people-and-organizational-performance/our-insights/linking-talent-to-value.

4   Verne Harnish, *Scaling up: How to Build a Meaningful Business ... and Enjoy the Ride* (New York: Gazelles, Inc, 2014).

clarity, as it breaks down functional accountabilities, required skills, traits, competencies, metrics, KPIs, and core values. It includes a rating scale that helps assess candidates during interviews, giving a clear picture of their strengths and weaknesses about the job requirements. Adapted from Geoff Smart's work, the scoreboard (learn more at geoffsmart.com/smarttool) not only helps identify top candidates but also provides valuable insights during onboarding. Identifying areas where a new hire may need additional support ensures a smoother transition and sets the stage for success. It's also an effective follow-up tool for a ninety-day performance review, allowing managers to measure progress and improvement from the initial assessment.

Moreover, ongoing communication and feedback are essential in maintaining role clarity. As roles evolve, regular check-ins provide opportunities to adjust expectations, refine goals, and address any challenges. This kind of dialogue not only reinforces the role's purpose but also nurtures a supportive work environment, which is critical for employee engagement and retention.

Ultimately, when roles are clearly defined and supported by consistent communication, employees feel more secure, confident, and capable of fulfilling their responsibilities. This clarity not only benefits individual performance but also fosters a more collaborative and motivated team, driving the organization's overall success.

SALARY: GETTING IT RIGHT

Determining the right salary for a position is crucial for attracting and retaining top talent. Research consistently shows that compensation is one of the most important factors in job satisfaction and employee retention. For example, a recent study by SHRM found that 63 percent of employees ranked salary as their top priority when considering a job change, highlighting the need for competitive and fair compensation to keep employees engaged and motivated.[5]

To ensure that salary ranges are aligned with market expectations, I use two primary methods.

1. **Online Research:** I conduct online research using tools like Glassdoor and Indeed's salary tabs, which offer insights into industry averages and regional differences. While these resources can be helpful, they often present broad estimates that may not reflect the most current trends or the specific nuances of the position. For example, Glassdoor might list a wide range of roles, but it may not account for differences in company size, location, or additional benefits that could impact compensation.

---

5   CEBS Stephen Miller, "Why Pay Is Driving Employee Satisfaction," Welcome to SHRM, December 21, 2023, https://www.shrm.org/topics-tools/news/benefits-compensation/pay-driving-employee-satisfaction.

2. **Market Research:** To supplement online data, I conduct market research through direct conversations with candidates at different experience levels. During interviews, I ask about their salary expectations and what they hope to earn in their next role. This approach not only provides a clearer picture of the current market rate but also encourages transparency from the start. I often communicate the salary range early in the process, clarifying that the final offer will depend on experience and fit. This helps avoid misalignment later and ensures that both parties have realistic expectations.

In one instance, while recruiting for a rapidly growing tech company, I found that the salary data from online sources fell significantly short of candidate expectations. Many tech candidates, especially those with specialized skills, were asking for 10 to 20 percent more than the averages reported online. By gathering feedback from several interviews, I was able to revise the salary range upwards, ultimately leading to faster hires and better-qualified candidates who felt valued and fairly compensated. This experience reinforced the importance of not relying solely on online data, as real-time market feedback can often reveal gaps that are crucial to closing the deal with top talent.

Moreover, transparency about salary from the beginning of the hiring process fosters trust. Research from PayScale indicates that 82 percent of employees are more likely to trust their employers when salary ranges are clearly communicated upfront.[6] Establishing this transparency not only attracts candidates but also helps improve the candidate's experience. When candidates know where they stand, it reduces anxiety. It increases their engagement throughout the hiring process, as they feel the company is being upfront and fair about what's on offer.

Ultimately, getting a salary right is not just about offering a competitive number; it's about using the data to create an offer that aligns with the role's responsibilities, company budget, and the candidate's value. This process of gathering accurate, real-time data from multiple sources and transparent communication ensures that the salary offered is both fair and competitive, helping the organization attract and retain top talent who feel valued and motivated to contribute.

CONCLUSION: LAYING THE GROUNDWORK FOR STRONG TEAMS

In this chapter, we've delved into the fundamental aspects of successful hiring: crafting effective job descriptions, achieving role clarity, implementing

---

6   Amy Stewart, People believe they're underpaid: Our fair pay report stats, July 22, 2021, https://www.payscale.com/compensation-trends/most-people-believe-they-are-underpaid-even-when-they-arent/.

practical tools like the Job Scoreboard,[7] and determining competitive salaries. These components are not merely administrative tasks; they serve as the foundation for building a strong, engaged, and high-performing workforce.

Clearly defined roles are essential for setting realistic expectations, fostering accountability, and enhancing employee motivation. When team members know exactly what's expected of them, they're more likely to meet or exceed those expectations, contributing meaningfully to the organization's success. Tools like the Job Scoreboard can further refine this clarity, guiding both the hiring and onboarding processes to ensure new hires are set up for success from day one.

Establishing competitive and fair compensation is equally critical. Fair salaries attract top talent, reduce turnover, and demonstrate the company's commitment to valuing its employees. Transparent discussions about salary not only build trust but also align candidates' expectations with the realities of the role, contributing to long-term engagement and retention.

Together, these strategies create a structured and intentional hiring process that aligns with organizational goals, drives team performance, and supports sustainable growth. By laying this groundwork, companies can attract the right talent,

---

7   Verne Harnish, *Scaling up: How to Build a Meaningful Business …* *and Enjoy the Ride* (New York: Gazelles, Inc, 2014).

nurture their development, and create a cohesive, motivated team capable of achieving exceptional outcomes.

KEY TAKEAWAYS

- **Role Clarity Is Crucial:** Clearly defined roles and responsibilities form the foundation of effective hiring and employee satisfaction. A well-crafted job description sets expectations and ensures that new hires understand their responsibilities from day one, reducing confusion and increasing productivity.

- **Job Descriptions as Strategic Tools: A** job description is more than just a document—it's a strategic asset that accurately reflects the role's duties, qualifications, and company culture. Regular updates ensure relevance, helping to attract the right candidates and maintain alignment across the organization.

- **Competitive Salaries Matter:** Offering competitive salaries is critical to attracting and retaining top talent. Regular market research and an understanding of candidate expectations help ensure that compensation aligns with industry standards and remains appealing.

- **Stakeholder Involvement Enhances Accuracy:** Engaging key stakeholders, including current employees and hiring managers, in the creation and refinement of job descriptions ensures accuracy and relevance. This collaborative approach improves role clarity and the overall hiring process, leading to better outcomes.

- **Use Technology for Greater Efficiency:** Leveraging AI-powered tools and platforms like Glassdoor, LinkedIn, and Indeed enhances job descriptions and recruitment efforts. This not only makes postings more visible and attractive but also streamlines the hiring process by reaching a wider pool of candidates.

ACTION STEPS

Take a moment to assess whether the job descriptions within your organization are up-to-date, clear, and aligned with current expectations. Engaging with key stakeholders, including current role holders, is critical to refining these descriptions and ensuring alignment throughout your organization. Here are some key steps to take.

- **Review and Update Job Descriptions:** Assess and revise job descriptions to ensure they are comprehensive and accurately reflect current responsibilities. Include clear expectations, qualifications, and key metrics for success. Engage current employees to gather insights and refine content, which not only clarifies expectations but also attracts better-suited candidates.

- **Engage Key Stakeholders in Refinement:** Collaborate with hiring managers, role holders, and HR professionals to refine job descriptions. This process not only improves role clarity but also fosters a sense of ownership among team members, enhancing both employee satisfaction and effective hiring.

- **Benchmark Salaries Regularly:** Conduct regular salary research using online tools, market data, and direct candidate feedback to stay competitive. Adjust salary ranges to align with market trends and ensure that compensation packages are attractive to potential hires while retaining current employees.

- **Implement the Job Scoreboard:**[8] Consider using tools like the Job Scoreboard to break down functional accountabilities, traits, competencies, and KPIs for roles. Use this tool not only in the hiring process but also as part of onboarding and performance reviews, ensuring clear expectations and tracking progress over time.

- **Leverage AI Tools for Job Descriptions:** Use AI-powered tools from platforms like LinkedIn and

---

8   Verne Harnish, *Scaling up: How to Build a Meaningful Business ... and Enjoy the Ride* (New York: Gazelles, Inc, 2014).

Indeed to generate and refine job description language. These tools can enhance visibility, relevance, and attractiveness, helping you reach a broader and more qualified candidate pool.

By focusing on these takeaways and following these action steps, you'll be better equipped to build a strong, aligned, and motivated team that drives your company's success. Implementing these best practices not only strengthens your team but also contributes to the long-term sustainability and growth of your organization.

Chapter 2

Building a Winning Team: Attracting and Selecting Talent

"Talent wins games, but teamwork and intelligence win championships."

—MICHAEL JORDAN

Five years ago, I began my journey as an executive recruiter, stepping into the challenging yet rewarding world of matching top talent with companies across Arizona. The US labor market was booming, and the unemployment rate was just 3.5 percent—the lowest since 1969.[9] The competition for quality candidates was fierce, and I quickly realized the high stakes of finding and retaining the right

---

9   Roxanna Edwards, BLS, April 2020, https://www.bls.gov/opub/mlr/2020/article/pdf/job-market-remains-tight-in-2019-as-the-unemployment-rate-falls-to-its-lowest-level-since-1969.pdf.

people. The cost of recruiting, hiring, and training is not just financial; it's also a matter of time, culture, and momentum.

According to Gartner, 36 percent of HR leaders cite a lack of resources as a significant barrier to attracting top talent.[10] This makes it clear: hiring A-players from the start isn't just beneficial—it's essential for long-term success. But how do you find those A-players in a crowded, fast-paced job market? It's not just about filling roles; it's about strategically building a team that will drive your company's growth, innovation, and culture forward.

In this chapter, we'll dive into how to attract and select talent effectively with practical strategies that focus not only on skill but also on potential, passion, and cultural fit. You'll discover how to create a magnetic employer brand, write job descriptions that resonate with top candidates, and conduct interviews that reveal the true capabilities and motivations of your candidates.

Let's explore what it takes to build a winning team, one hire at a time.

---

10   Mary Baker, "Gartner HR Research Finds Organizations Are in the Midst of a Reset; Most Are Not Prepared," Gartner, October 28, 2024, https://www.gartner.com/en/newsroom/press-releases/2024-10-28-gartner-hr-research-finds-organizations-are-in-the-midst-of-a-reset-most-are-not-prepared.

THE COST OF HIRING AND RETAINING TALENT

The financial impact of hiring is significant, but it also affects team dynamics, momentum, and company culture. According to SHRM, onboarding a new employee costs an average of $4,100, though this can vary by industry and role.[11] In a 100-person organization with an average salary of $50,000, turnover and replacement costs can range from $660,000 to $2.6 million annually. Moreover, onboarding documents alone can cost up to $400 per employee for small to mid-sized businesses, and it can take a mid-level manager up to 6.2 months to reach full productivity.

These statistics emphasize the need for thoughtful hiring. The wrong hire doesn't just cost money—it can erode morale, disrupt workflows, and even cause top performers to leave. In contrast, finding the right hire not only enhances productivity but also fosters a positive, engaged culture.

ATTRACTING TOP TALENT

Attracting top talent requires more than just a job posting—it's about presenting your company as an attractive and inspiring place to work. Successful strategies in today's competitive market focus on flexibility, employer branding, career development, and fostering a positive work environment.

---

11   Katie Navarra, "The Real Costs of Recruitment," Welcome to SHRM, December 21, 2023, https://www.shrm.org/topics-tools/news/talent-acquisition/real-costs-recruitment.

- **The Power of Flexibility:** Offering flexibility has become essential to attracting high-quality candidates. In a LinkedIn survey I conducted in August 2023, nearly half of the respondents favored a hybrid work schedule, while another 45 percent preferred remote work. Only 7 percent wanted to be onsite full-time. These findings align with broader trends, as seen in a Statista survey where 58 percent of respondents reported improved job satisfaction due to flexible working arrangements.[12]

The option for hybrid or remote work is not just a perk—it's a competitive advantage. For example, the gradual increase of in-office days over time allows new hires to acclimate to the company culture while maintaining the flexibility they value. In the UK, experiments with a four-day workweek have shown significant benefits in productivity and employee motivation. A Gallup poll further found that 76 percent of workers would be more likely to stay with their current employer if offered flexible hours, demonstrating the clear link between flexibility and retention.[13]

---

12   Raphael Bohne, "Flexible Workspace: Benefits 2018," Statista, July 6, 2022, https://www.statista.com/statistics/980129/flexible-workspace-effects-worldwide/.

13   Lydia Saad and Ben Wigert, "Remote Work Persisting and Trending Permanent," Gallup.com, October 16, 2024, https://news.gallup.com/poll/355907/remote-work-persisting-trending-permanent.aspx.

- **Building a Magnetic Employer Brand:** Your employer brand is more than just a logo or tagline; it's the embodiment of your company's culture, values, and mission. Companies like McDonald's or Tesla benefit from strong, established brands that naturally attract candidates. However, for smaller businesses, the challenge lies in cultivating a positive reputation from the ground up.

A strong employer brand can be built through authentic storytelling, employee testimonials, and a professional online presence across platforms like LinkedIn, Glassdoor, and your company website. Positive reviews and active engagement on social media are crucial for boosting credibility. Your current employees can be powerful advocates; satisfied team members are likely to refer their network, bringing in like-minded, qualified candidates who align with the company culture.

- **Career Development as a Recruitment Tool:** Top performers seek environments where they can grow, learn, and advance. Providing clear paths for development not only attracts ambitious candidates but also retains them. Regular discussions about career goals, mentorship opportunities, and alignment with company objectives can help employees envision a future with your organization. For instance, when employees express interest in promotions or raises, offering small projects aligned with company goals can help them build the necessary skills.

STRATEGIES FOR ATTRACTING TALENT

Attracting the right talent involves a blend of branding, compensation, development opportunities, and a positive candidate experience. Here's how to refine your approach.

- **Develop a Strong Employer Brand:** Your employer brand is the beacon that draws talent to your organization. It's more than just a logo or a tagline; it's the embodiment of your company's culture, values, and mission. When these elements are clearly communicated and consistently portrayed, they resonate with candidates who share similar beliefs and aspirations. A strong employer brand doesn't just attract candidates—it attracts the right candidates. These are individuals who are not only qualified but also aligned with your company's vision, making them more likely to thrive and contribute positively to your workplace.

- **Offer Competitive Compensation and Benefits:** In today's market, competitive compensation is more than just a salary number. It's about offering a comprehensive package that meets the diverse needs of your employees. This includes attractive salaries, performance bonuses, healthcare options, retirement plans, and, increasingly, flexible work arrangements. When candidates see that your company values their well-being and future, they're more likely to view your organization as a desirable place to grow their careers. Remember, top talent has choices—ensuring your compensation and benefits package stands out can be the key to securing their commitment.

- **Provide Learning and Development Opportunities:** Ambitious professionals are drawn to opportunities where they can grow, learn, and advance. By investing in training programs, mentorship, and clear career progression paths, you position your company as a place where employees can build a future. Whether it's through formal education, on-the-job training, or leadership development programs, offering these opportunities signals to candidates that your organization is committed to their long-term success. This can be a significant differentiator in attracting talent who are eager to develop their skills and advance their careers.

- **Foster a Diverse and Inclusive Workplace:** A truly successful organization values diversity and inclusion—not just in words but in action. Creating a workplace where every employee feels valued, respected, and included fosters innovation and drives success. Emphasize these values in your hiring practices, showcasing your commitment to building a diverse team. This approach not only broadens your talent pool but also attracts candidates who value inclusivity and seek a workplace where they can bring their whole selves to work.

- **Leverage Social Media and Online Platforms:** In an age where social media is a powerful tool for brand communication, your company's online presence can be a game-changer in attracting talent. Utilize platforms like LinkedIn, Facebook, and Instagram to showcase your company's strengths, share employee stories, and highlight your organizational culture. Regular, engaging content that speaks to your company's values and successes can turn passive job seekers into active candidates. By creating an interactive and informative social media presence, you not only attract candidates but also build a community around your brand.

- **Encourage Employee Referrals:** Your current employees are your best ambassadors. Encourage them to refer qualified candidates by creating a referral program that rewards successful hires. Employees who are satisfied with their jobs are likely to recommend others who would be a good fit, ensuring a better cultural match. This strategy often leads to high-quality hires, as referred candidates come with a personal endorsement, reducing the risk of a bad fit. Plus, it fosters a sense of involvement and investment among your current workforce.

- **Create a Positive Candidate Experience:** The candidate experience reflects your company's values and professionalism. From the first contact to the final decision, ensure that every interaction is respectful, timely, and transparent. Effective communication throughout the hiring process—whether it's providing feedback, answering questions, or keeping candidates informed—can significantly enhance their perception of your company. A positive candidate's experience not only increases the likelihood of securing top talent but also boosts your company's reputation in the broader job market.

- **Offer Flexible Work Arrangements:** The pandemic has reshaped the workplace, making flexibility a top priority for many job seekers. Offering options such as remote work, hybrid schedules, or flexible hours can set your company apart from competitors. Today's employees value the ability to balance work with personal life, and offering this flexibility shows that you understand and respect their needs. By embracing these changes, your company not only meets the expectations of modern candidates but also positions itself as a forward-thinking employer.

- **Showcase Company Culture Through Content:** To attract the right talent, you need to give them a reason to choose you over the competition. One effective way to do this is by showcasing your company culture through authentic content—blogs, videos, and employee testimonials. A well-placed video on your careers page can feature employees discussing their roles, sharing what they love about working at your company, and highlighting the unique aspects of your workplace. This not only excites potential candidates but also helps them envision themselves as part of your team. For harder-to-fill positions, consider a "day in the life" video that offers a detailed look at the role, helping candidates better understand what the job entails.

- **Participate in Industry Events and Job Fairs:** Engaging directly with potential candidates through industry events, conferences, and job fairs can be a highly effective recruitment strategy. These events offer opportunities to network, showcase your company, and attract candidates who are actively seeking new opportunities. By having a presence at these events, you position your company as a leader in your field and create personal connections with candidates who are genuinely interested in your industry.

SELECTION PROCESS

Attracting candidates is only the first step; selecting the right talent is equally critical. An effective selection process requires structured interviews, data-driven recruitment, pre-employment assessments, and thorough reference checks.

- **Structured Interviews and Assessments:** Structured interviews, where candidates are evaluated based on consistent criteria, help reduce bias and improve decision-making. Using tools like Applicant Tracking Systems (ATS) streamlines the process and manages candidate communication more effectively. Additionally, pre-employment assessments that evaluate skills, cultural fit, and cognitive abilities provide further insights into candidates' suitability for the role. While these assessments offer valuable data, it's essential to balance them with human intuition.

- **Thorough Candidate Evaluation:** The candidate evaluation process is like perfecting a recipe: miss an ingredient, and the dish won't come together. Recruiters are your front line, sifting through resumes and profiles to find the best candidates. During phone screenings, recruiters should look beyond surface qualifications and dig deeper. For instance, one recruiter I worked with discovered a candidate's knack for process automation, which wasn't on their resume but aligned perfectly with the company's needs.

Reference checks, often seen as a formality, are the final frontier in candidate evaluation. These conversations should be thorough and focused, asking questions about job responsibilities, areas for growth, and work style. By approaching reference checks with curiosity and open-ended questions, you can uncover deeper insights into a candidate's potential fit.

- **Candidate Evaluation Stage:** Once you've successfully attracted a pool of qualified candidates, it's time to dive into the critical evaluation process. This is where the magic happens—or where the reality check begins. A comprehensive evaluation process is like crafting the perfect gourmet meal: miss an ingredient, and the whole dish could flop. Whether you're aiming for a perfectly cooked steak or a mouthwatering vegan delight, the secret is in getting the recipe just right.

THE CANDIDATE SELECTION PROCESS

Here's how to ensure your candidate selection process is as satisfying as your favorite dish—be it filet mignon or a delightful portobello mushroom steak.

1. Recruiter Engagement: The First Line of Defense

Recruiters are your frontline warriors in the battle for talent. They sift through resumes, LinkedIn profiles, and initial communications like detectives searching for clues. The key here is not just to spot the obvious qualifications but to dig deeper. Is there a hidden potential for innovation or a cultural fit that might not be immediately apparent?

For example, I once worked with a recruiter who, during a quick phone screening, noticed that a candidate casually mentioned a side project where they had automated a tedious task at their previous job. This wasn't mentioned anywhere on their resume. Intrigued, the recruiter dug deeper and discovered that the candidate had a knack for streamlining processes—a skill that perfectly aligned with the company's drive for efficiency. However, the recruiter also considered how this process-oriented mindset would fit into the company's existing culture. In this case, the deeper conversation revealed a hidden gem that wasn't obvious from the resume alone and showed that the candidate's approach could enhance the team's dynamic.

- **Pro Tip:** Encourage your recruiters to be curious—ask questions, look for connections, and never underestimate the power of a well-crafted LinkedIn summary. Sometimes, the best candidates are those who don't fit the mold perfectly but bring something unique to the table, blending innovation with a cultural fit that can take your team to the next level.

2. Assessments: The Crystal Ball of Hiring

Assessments are like your hiring crystal ball—they help you peer into the candidate's future performance. But beware, not all assessments are created equal. To truly understand a candidate's potential, you'll need a mix of tools.

- **Cultural Fit:** Do they mesh well with your company's values, or are they more likely to stir the pot? Cultural fit is crucial—think of it as the seasoning that makes all the ingredients work together.

- **Behavioral Assessments:** Past behavior is often the best predictor of future performance. At a tech company I consulted for, a behavioral assessment revealed that a candidate who was initially seen as a strong contender might struggle with the fast-paced, high-pressure environment. This insight helped the hiring team make a more informed decision.

- **Aptitude Tests:** These measure the candidate's ability to learn and adapt—because no one wants to hire someone who can't keep up with the times.

- **Skills Assessments:** Whether they're a coding wizard or a communication guru, it's essential to know exactly what skills the candidate brings to the table. Don't just take their word for it—test it!

- **Pro Tip:** Assessments are great, but don't let them overshadow human intuition. Use them as a tool, not a crutch. And remember, there's no assessment for "gut feeling"—trust yours.

3. Career History Review: The Detective Work

Peering into a candidate's past can feel a bit like being Sherlock Holmes, except instead of a magnifying glass, you've got a resume in one hand and a LinkedIn profile in the other. But don't stop at surface-level observations—dig deeper.

- **Reasons for Leaving Previous Jobs:** If they've jumped ship a few times, find out why. I once reviewed the career history of a candidate who had left three jobs in as many years. While this initially seemed concerning, a deeper look revealed that each move was for legitimate reasons—better opportunities and career growth. This context changed the narrative from "job hopper" to "ambitious and career-focused."

- **Industry Experience:** How well do they know the field? Are they a seasoned veteran or a promising rookie? Understanding their experience in your industry helps set realistic expectations.

- **Pro Tip:** Don't shy away from asking tough questions. Understanding the story behind a candidate's career moves can reveal a lot about their motivations and long-term potential.

4. Candidate Engagement: The Real Talk

This is where the rubber meets the road. Engaging directly with the candidate allows you to move beyond paper qualifications and get to the heart of what makes them tick.

- **Share the Employer Value Proposition:** What's your company's secret sauce? Clearly communicate what makes your company unique and why the candidate should want to be part of your team.

- **Understand the Candidate's Motivations:** Why are they interested in this role? During a phone conversation, a candidate once revealed that their primary motivation was finding a workplace with strong mentorship. This insight allowed us to tailor the role to include mentorship opportunities, making the position more attractive to them.

- **Answer Questions and Encourage Next Steps:** Provide clarity on the role and ask the candidate to proceed to the next stage if they're a good fit. This not only reassures the candidate but also sets clear expectations for the process.

- **Pro Tip:** Don't just sell the job—sell the experience. Candidates are looking for more than just a paycheck; they're looking for a place where they can grow, thrive, and make a difference.

5. Reference Checks: The Final Level of Hiring

Reference checks are like reaching the final level of a video game—if you've made it this far, you're close to the finish line, but a few key challenges remain. It's crucial to approach this stage with care and precision to ensure a thorough assessment of the candidate.

- **Candidate-Provided Contacts**: Ask candidates to provide contact information for two to three professional references, ideally including past supervisors, peers, and, if applicable, subordinates. This helps you gather a well-rounded view of the candidate's work style and leadership abilities.

- **Recruiter-Initiated Outreach**: Have the recruiter initiate contact via text to schedule a convenient time for the reference check. This not only respects the reference's time but also sets the tone for a productive conversation.

- **Concise Questionnaire**: Prepare a one-page questionnaire to guide the conversation. Focus on key questions such as.

1. How long did you work together?

2. What was your professional relationship (e.g., supervisor, peer)?

3. What were the candidate's primary responsibilities?

4. What did they excel at in their role?

5. Were there areas they were working to improve?

6. How did they handle feedback and constructive criticism?

7. Can you describe their leadership or teamwork style?

8. Would you work with this person again?

- **Conducting the Interview**: Use the questionnaire as a guide during the reference check, but be flexible enough to explore additional insights. This structured yet adaptable approach ensures you obtain consistent and relevant information across all references.

- **Pro Tip**: References aren't just a box to check—they're an opportunity to get the inside scoop on a candidate. Listen actively, ask follow-up questions, and dig deeper to uncover valuable insights.

By following these steps, you'll ensure a comprehensive candidate evaluation process that not only identifies the best fit for your organization but also aligns with your company's values and culture. Remember, the goal isn't just to fill a position—it's to find someone who will thrive in your environment and contribute to your team's long-term success.

Through countless hires and many lessons learned, I've found that the candidate evaluation stage is where the real work begins. It's not just about checking boxes—it's about understanding the person behind the resume and how they'll fit into your company's unique ecosystem.

CONCLUSION: YOUR STRATEGIC APPROACH

Attracting and selecting the right talent is a strategic and deliberate process in building a winning team. It goes beyond simply filling a vacancy; it's about finding individuals who align with your company's values, culture, and vision for growth. As we've explored in this chapter, the path to finding top talent is layered with intentional efforts, from creating a compelling employer brand to offering competitive benefits, ensuring flexibility, and fostering a positive candidate experience.

Once you've attracted a talented pool, a structured selection process is essential to evaluate candidates holistically. By combining assessments, in-depth interviews, and thorough reference checks, you create a multi-dimensional view of each candidate's potential and cultural fit. The aim is not just to find someone with the right skills but to identify those who will thrive within your team and contribute meaningfully to your organization's future.

Building a successful team takes time, but every intentional hire strengthens your foundation for long-term success. Thoughtful hiring is not only an investment in skills but also in the innovation, engagement, and cohesion that these individuals bring to the workplace. As Michael Jordan's words remind us, "Talent wins games, but teamwork and intelligence win championships." With each strategic hire, you're building a team equipped to drive growth, meet challenges, and contribute to the company's vision.

With your ideal candidates identified, the next step is crucial: mastering the interview process. In Chapter 3, we'll dive into strategies and techniques for conducting interviews that reveal true potential, align with organizational goals, and ensure a seamless transition from candidate to team member.

KEY TAKEAWAYS

- **Strategic Recruitment Is Essential:** Attracting and selecting the right talent is not just about filling positions but about building a strong, capable team that aligns with your company's values and goals.

- **Flexibility Is a Competitive Advantage:** Offering flexible work arrangements can set your company apart and attract top talent in today's evolving job market.

- **Branding Matters:** A strong employer brand, backed by authentic content and a positive online presence, is crucial for attracting candidates who resonate with your company's mission.

- **Invest in Development:** Providing clear paths for career advancement and continuous learning is key to attracting ambitious professionals who want to grow with your organization.

- **Thorough Candidate Evaluation Is Key:** A well-rounded candidate evaluation process, incorporating recruiter insights, assessments, career history, candidate engagement, and reference checks, is essential for making informed hiring decisions that align with your company's long-term goals.

ACTION STEPS

- **Audit Your Employer Brand:** Evaluate your current employer branding efforts. Does your company's online presence, including your website and social media profiles, accurately reflect your culture and values? Identify areas where you can enhance your brand to attract the right candidates better.

- **Implement Flexible Work Arrangements:** If you haven't already, consider offering flexible work options such as remote work, hybrid schedules, or adjustable hours. Survey your current employees to understand their preferences and incorporate flexibility into your recruitment strategy to attract top talent.

- **Enhance Your Recruitment Process with Technology:** Explore Applicant Tracking Systems (ATS) and other recruitment technologies that can streamline your hiring process, reduce bias, and provide data-driven insights. Implementing these tools can help you improve efficiency and make more informed hiring decisions.

- **Foster a Diverse and Inclusive Workplace:** Assess your hiring practices to ensure they promote diversity and inclusion. Implement strategies to attract a broader range of candidates and create a welcoming environment where all employees feel valued.

- **Refine Candidate Evaluation:** Develop a comprehensive candidate evaluation process that includes recruiter engagement, assessments, career history reviews, direct candidate engagement, and thorough reference checks. This holistic approach ensures that you don't just fill a position but find someone who will thrive in your environment and contribute to your team's long-term success.

Attracting and selecting the right talent is a multifaceted process that involves much more than simply filling a vacancy. By understanding the costs associated with hiring and retention, implementing strategies to enhance flexibility, employer branding, and career development, and rigorously evaluating candidates, you can significantly increase your chances of attracting top performers. The candidate evaluation stage is particularly crucial, as it allows you to assess not only the qualifications but also the cultural fit of potential hires. A strategic approach to recruitment benefits your organization by improving productivity and retention and ensures that you build a strong, capable team poised for long-term success.

Chapter 3

Mastering the Interview Process

"In looking for people to hire, you look for three qualities: integrity, intelligence, and energy. And if they don't have the first, the other two will kill you. The interview is where you learn whether they have all three."

—WARREN BUFFETT

THE IMPACT OF A POORLY EXECUTED INTERVIEW PROCESS

To kick things off, let me share a story that captures what can go wrong in an interview process. A candidate, eager and well-prepared, arrived at a reputable company expecting a structured evaluation. However, with each successive interviewer, she was asked the same question: *"Tell me about yourself."* By the third repetition, frustration set in. She wondered if anyone had reviewed her resume or prepared for the interview. The redundancy wasn't just an annoyance; it signaled disorganization, misalignment among interviewers, and a lack of internal communication. No new information was gathered, and it was clear the interviewers weren't aligned. The candidate felt undervalued and disengaged—and she ultimately declined the job offer.

This story illustrates the need for a well-coordinated, layered interview approach. In today's competitive market, candidates have options, and a lackluster interview process can quickly turn away top talent. In fact, 83 percent of candidates surveyed by LinkedIn stated that a negative interview experience could change their opinion of a company they once liked, while 87 percent said a positive experience could make them reconsider a role they had doubts about.[14]

THE IMPORTANCE OF A LAYERED APPROACH

An effective interview process isn't about rapid-fire questions or rushing through rounds; it's about uncovering new insights at each stage. Different interviewers should focus on distinct aspects, each tied to their role and future interaction with the candidate. This structure not only prevents

---

14   "Candidate Experience Statistics 2024: Regularly Updated," Stand-Out CV | Create a winning CV in minutes with our simple CV builder, August 5, 2024, https://standout-cv.com/candidate-experience-statistics.

redundancy but also helps paint a fuller picture of the candidate.

One of my clients, for example, overhauled their process to include a "final culture check" with the CEO. The initial rounds focused on competency, team dynamics, and role expectations, while the CEO's interview centered on cultural fit, strategic vision, and potential growth. This approach improved hiring outcomes, allowing the company to identify candidates who could not only perform the job but elevate it. The candidate also left the interview feeling valued, respected, and clear about the company's expectations.

STORY SPOTLIGHT: THE IMPACT OF LAYERED INTERVIEWS

A mid-sized tech company I worked with once struggled with high turnover, especially in technical roles. Upon examining their interview process, we discovered that it lacked a structured approach, often resulting in mismatches between the hired candidate and the team culture. We decided to implement a three-tier interview strategy.

1. **The first round** focused on cultural alignment, where HR assessed the candidate's long-term goals, values, and motivations.

2. **The second round** was a technical interview led by a senior engineer designed to test problem-solving abilities.

3. **The final round** featured a meeting with the CEO to discuss the company's vision, growth plans, and long-term fit.

Within six months of implementing this layered approach, the company's retention rate improved by 40 percent, and the new hires began contributing innovative ideas almost immediately. This success story underscores how a well-designed interview process can be a game-changer.

WHY COMMUNICATION MATTERS

Clear communication is the backbone of an effective interview process. Sharing notes among interviewers, defining roles in advance, and aligning on what to focus on not only streamline the process but also demonstrate the company's professionalism. A well-structured, communicative approach inspires confidence and ensures that candidates feel informed and respected.

Consider this: 55 percent of job seekers abandon the application process if they experience poor communication during interviews.[15] It's not just

---

15   Shelby Palmeri Farris, "2024 Candidate Experience Report," CareerPlug, February 2, 2024, https://www.careerplug.com/blog/candidate-experience-statistics/.

about gathering information—it's about providing a seamless candidate experience that reflects the company's culture. When candidates see a professional, coordinated process, they're more likely to envision themselves in a well-organized, efficient work environment.

REFLECTING ON COMMON PITFALLS

Reflecting on past mistakes can be as valuable as celebrating wins. Think back to the first story—redundant questions, misaligned interviewers, and frustrated candidates. These issues aren't rare; they're common pitfalls that can lead to lost opportunities, rushed decisions, and cultural mismatches.

Poor communication, a lack of preparation, and inconsistent questioning can cost more than just time; they can cost you top talent. One global study by CareerBuilder found that bad hires cost organizations an average of $15,000 per hire.[16] A poorly executed interview process is one of the leading causes.

Take a moment to reflect on your own hiring practices. Are there aspects you wish to improve? What common mistakes do you encounter? Jot down

---

16   Ladan Nikravan Hayes, "Nearly Three in Four Employers Affected by a Bad Hire, According to a Recent CareerBuilder Survey," Press Room | Career Builder, December 7, 2017, https://press.careerbuilder.com/2017-12-07-Nearly-Three-in-Four-Employers-Affected-by-a-Bad-Hire-According-to-a-Recent-CareerBuilder-Survey.

a couple of thoughts—you'll find them useful as we continue exploring this chapter.

THE SIX-STEP INTERVIEW PROCESS

To build an effective interview process, you need a structured yet adaptable approach. Here's a deeper dive into each step.

1. **Sourcing**: This is where it all starts. Define the role's requirements and qualifications clearly, create an engaging job description, and post it across various channels while actively sourcing passive candidates.

2. **Application Review**: As applications come in, review resumes and credentials thoroughly, focusing on specific skills and experiences that align with the role.

3. **Pre-Screening**: Conduct pre-screen calls to verify qualifications, clarify role expectations, and gauge initial cultural fit. This step helps filter candidates before the more intensive interviews.

4. **Virtual Interviews**: Zoom or video interviews allow you to assess the candidate's communication style, competencies, and personality. This is also where you can test the candidate's adaptability, especially if the role involves remote collaboration.

5. **In-Person Interviews**: This step provides deeper insights into how candidates interact with the team and whether their potential fit within the physical work environment. Use behavioral and situational questions to gauge how they'll handle real-life challenges.

6. **The Job Offer**: After selecting the best candidate, extend a verbal offer, followed by a written one. Be transparent about salary, benefits, and role expectations to prevent surprises.

UNDERSTANDING THE INTERVIEW PROCESS: IT'S MORE THAN A MEETING

The interview process is more than just a series of meetings. It's an opportunity to represent your company's mission, values, and culture. Effective interviews can lead to the formation of cohesive teams, drive innovation, and contribute to the overall success of your organization.

STORY SPOTLIGHT: THE TURNAROUND MANAGER

I once consulted for a department with a turnover problem. Exit interviews revealed that poor hiring decisions were to blame—candidates often lacked cultural fit or key competencies. We revamped the interview process, adding structured behavioral and values-based questions. Within a year, turnover dropped by 30 percent, and team performance surged. It was a clear reminder: a strategic interview process not only fills vacancies but also fosters team harmony and reduces costly turnover.

TYPES OF INTERVIEW QUESTIONS: FINDING THE RIGHT FIT

A well-rounded interview process involves using various types of questions.

- **Behavioral Questions**: These questions explore past experiences to predict future performance.

  o Example: *"Tell me about a time when you faced a significant challenge at work. How did you handle it, and what was the outcome?"*

- **Competency-Based Questions**: These focus on specific skills and competencies.

  o Example: *"Describe a project where you used problem-solving skills to overcome an obstacle. What steps did you take?"*

- **Values-Based Questions**: These determine alignment with company culture.

  o Example: *"How do you approach collaboration with colleagues from different departments? Can you provide an example of your contribution to a team effort?"*

- **Open vs. Closed Questions**: Open questions, like *"What motivates you to do your best work?"* provide detailed insights. Closed questions, such as *"Are you comfortable working onsite five days a week?"* confirm specific facts. Using a mix of these questions not only provides a comprehensive understanding of the candidate's abilities and values but also ensures that the process is thorough and fair.

WHY INTERVIEW SKILLS MATTER FOR MANAGERS

Interview skills are essential for any manager aiming to build high-performing teams. Effective interviewing can lead to better talent acquisition, enhanced team performance, and reduced turnover. By honing these skills, managers can ensure a good fit, foster collaboration, and contribute to long-term success.

POST-INTERVIEW PROCEDURES: DON'T DROP THE BALL

Once the interviews are complete, the process isn't over. The post-interview phase is crucial for informed decision-making and maintaining a positive candidate experience.

- **Provide Prompt Feedback**: Follow up with the recruiter within 24 to 48 hours to keep the process moving and maintain candidate engagement.

- **Collaborate Consistently**: Maintain clear communication between the recruiter and hiring manager, refining the search if needed.

- **Make Timely Decisions**: Avoid delays that could lead to losing top candidates to competitors.

CONCLUSION: IT'S ABOUT BUILDING EXTRAORDINARY TEAMS

In this chapter, we've explored the importance of mastering the interview process, a pivotal step in building high-performing, cohesive teams that embody your company's values and drive its mission forward. A well-structured interview process is more than just assessing skills; it's about uncovering integrity, alignment with your company's culture, and potential for growth—qualities that ensure each new hire doesn't just fill a role but enriches your organization.

From pre-screening to in-depth interviews, each step presents an opportunity to showcase your company's commitment to excellence, offering candidates a clear, respectful, and engaging experience. As we discussed, a layered approach brings fresh insights at every stage, allowing you to see a fuller picture of each candidate's strengths, values, and fit.

Clear communication and intentional coordination among interviewers are critical to avoiding common missteps like redundancy and misalignment, which can turn away top talent. When candidates experience a smooth, professional process, they're more likely to envision themselves as part of an organized, intentional workplace. Thoughtful questions and respectful follow-up reinforce your brand, enhance the candidate experience, and ultimately strengthen your hiring outcomes.

Mastering the interview process is about more than filling seats—it's about laying a foundation for long-term success. In small to midsize businesses, each hire can profoundly impact culture and performance. By refining each phase of your hiring process, you not only bring in talent that will contribute today but also foster a culture that will sustain growth, innovation, and cohesion.

In the next section, we'll dive into the art of inspiring and retaining your team, creating an environment where every employee feels valued, supported, and motivated to give their best. After all, hiring is just the beginning; building a workplace where people thrive is the true measure of a successful organization.

KEY TAKEAWAYS

- **Structure and Strategy Matter:** Effective interviews require planning, clear objectives, and strategic questioning to uncover the right talent.

- **Communication Is Key:** Maintain open lines of communication throughout the process to ensure a positive candidate experience and well-informed hiring decisions.

- **Continuous Improvement:** Reflect on your current interview practices and identify areas for improvement to continually enhance your approach.

ACTION STEPS

- **Review Your Current Interview Process:** Identify any gaps or weaknesses and develop a plan to address them.

- **Train Your Team:** Ensure all interviewers are well-prepared and understand their roles and objectives in the interview process.

- **Gather Feedback:** After each interview cycle, gather feedback from both interviewers and candidates to refine and improve your process.

By understanding and implementing these principles, you can make informed hiring decisions that contribute to your company's long-term success. Remember, the interview process is your opportunity to build not just a team but a community of dedicated, engaged, and high-performing professionals. Next, we'll explore company culture, building trust, and maintaining a connection.

OVERVIEW OF PART 2: INSPIRE (FOCUS: MOTIVATION AND EMPOWERMENT)

- **Chapter 4: Creating a Culture of Recognition**

    o **Performance/Communication:** This chapter focuses on using clear communication to recognize employees' achievements, helping them align with the company's mission and values.

- **Chapter 5: Empowering Leadership and Growth**

    o **Purpose, Mission, Vision, and Values:** This section outlines how reinforcing the company's purpose and values inspires leadership and growth in employees—the emphasis on authentic leadership and the impact of aligning personal and professional goals.

- **Chapter 6: Building Trust and Connection**

    o **Branding Strategy:** Branding equals' trust. This section explores how when employees connect to the company's brand, they will feel pride in representing the organization. This chapter emphasizes how clear and consistent messaging not only builds customer trust but also fosters employee loyalty and engagement, tying it back to retention and motivation.

As we move from hiring to inspiring, the focus shifts toward building an environment where employees feel recognized, empowered, and connected to the company's vision. Attracting the right talent is only the first step; sustaining motivation and fostering growth within your team is essential for long-term success. In "INSPIRE," we'll explore how to cultivate a culture that celebrates achievements, promotes authentic leadership, and strengthens the bonds between employees and the company's brand. By creating this foundation, your organization not only retains top talent but also drives a deeper sense of purpose and pride, setting the stage for sustained engagement and loyalty.

PART 2

Inspire

Focus: Motivation and Empowerment

"Everyone talks about building a relationship with your customer. I think you build one with your employees first. When people feel valued, trusted, and connected, that's when the culture thrives, and growth follows."

—ANGELA AHRENDTS

About a decade ago, I visited a company where every employee, from entry-level to executive, felt valued and empowered. There was palpable energy and dedication in the air—a culture where people were motivated not just by their roles but by their purpose within the organization. It was clear that this wasn't just a job for them; it was a place where they felt connected, recognized, and driven to grow.

Creating such an environment is no accident. It's built through intentional leadership, a commitment to recognizing individual and team achievements, and an authentic, people-centered brand that resonates from the inside out. While hiring the right talent sets the foundation, keeping them inspired requires a commitment to ongoing growth, fostering trust, and creating a space where people feel safe to innovate and take ownership.

In this section, we'll explore how to cultivate a culture of recognition that celebrates contributions big and small, a leadership approach that nurtures growth, and an employer brand that reflects your values and invites trust and connection. Motivation and empowerment aren't just strategies; they're the heart of a thriving organization.

As we begin Chapter 4, "Creating a Culture of Recognition and Growth," we'll dive into the practices and mindsets that help build a workplace where people are not only motivated to excel but empowered to contribute their best. Let's embark on the journey of inspiring a culture that fuels both individual and organizational success.

Chapter 4

Creating a Culture of Recognition

"Businesses often forget about the culture, and ultimately, they suffer for it because you can't deliver good service from unhappy employees."

—TONY HSIEH

A company's culture of recognition is one of the most powerful motivators for its employees. Recognition goes beyond financial rewards—it's about creating an environment where achievements, strengths, and contributions are acknowledged, and employees feel seen and valued. When this type of culture thrives, it lays the foundation for trust, clear communication, and overall organizational success. More importantly, recognition sets the stage for leadership development and growth, which will be explored in the following chapter.

THE IMPORTANCE OF RECOGNITION

Recognition is a vital element of employee engagement and retention, as supported by various studies. According to Gallup, organizations that prioritize regular recognition experience a 21 percent increase in productivity and 22 percent higher profitability.[17] Additionally, research from the Society for Human Resource Management (SHRM) indicates that companies with strong recognition programs enjoy 31 percent lower turnover rates.[18] These statistics reveal the tangible benefits of consistent appreciation: employees who feel valued are more likely to be committed and productive.

The psychological benefits are equally compelling. A study from the University of Massachusetts found that employees who feel recognized are three times more likely to be motivated and report higher job satisfaction.[19] When organizations integrate structured recognition into their culture, they not

---

17   Esq. Danielle M. Jones, "The 48 Employee Recognition Statistics to Take Note of in 2024 - SSR," RSS, March 27, 2024, https://www.selectsoftwarereviews.com/blog/employee-recognition-statistics.

18   Esq. Danielle M. Jones, "The 48 Employee Recognition Statistics to Take Note of in 2024 - SSR," RSS, March 27, 2024, https://www.selectsoftwarereviews.com/blog/employee-recognition-statistics.

19   Esq. Danielle M. Jones, "The 48 Employee Recognition Statistics to Take Note of in 2024 - SSR," RSS, March 27, 2024, https://www.selectsoftwarereviews.com/blog/employee-recognition-statistics.

only foster a positive work environment but also improve employee commitment and performance.

REAL ESTATE DEVELOPMENT COMPANY CASE STUDY: MINTO GROUP

Let's look at a real-world example: Minto Group, a real estate development company, faced challenges in creating a culture of recognition.[20] Historically, the company's culture did not prioritize acknowledgment, with managers often perceiving recognition as unnecessary for employees simply doing their jobs. This resulted in a culture where appreciation was infrequent, causing disengagement and isolation, especially given the dispersed nature of the workforce across job sites and corporate offices.

To address these issues, Minto launched BRAVO!, a formal recognition platform optimized using software like Bonusly, Workhuman, and Kudos.[21] This platform enabled employees to give each other meaningful recognition, boosting morale and creating a more connected workplace. Within three months, 60 percent of employees had received recognition, demonstrating the program's immediate impact.[22]

20   Sarah Mulcahy, "Bringing Recognition to Real Estate: Minto Group's Story," LinkedIn, March 10, 2018, https://www.linkedin.com/pulse/bringing-recognition-real-estate-minto-groups-story-sarah-payne/.
21   Live more by Minto - blog | A guide to living your best life, December 9, 2022, https://www.minto.com/live-more-blog/index.html.
22   Our employees | more with minto | 2023 ESG report, accessed November 5, 2024, https://www.minto.com/minto-green/Community-Impact-Our-Employees~1832.html.

Managers also used data from the platform to track recognition's effectiveness and its influence on performance, ultimately modernizing the company's culture and increasing employee engagement.

This case demonstrates how investing in a structured recognition system can quickly transform a disconnected culture into a more positive, engaged environment.

BUILDING RECOGNITION OF THE COMPANY'S DAILY RHYTHM

There must be regular opportunities for feedback, appreciation, and professional development to build a sustainable culture of recognition. Here's how this can be effectively embedded into the daily workflow.

- **One-on-One Weekly Meetings:** These sessions provide opportunities to coach employees, give feedback, and track progress. A clear agenda and consistent structure create space for meaningful conversations that build trust and promote personal growth.

- **Mid-Year and Annual Reviews:** These structured sessions go beyond day-to-day tasks, focusing on career development, goal setting, and gathering insights on the employee experience. Consistent check-ins establish a culture of feedback and ensure alignment with company goals.

- **Performance Improvement Plans (PIPs) and Terminations:** Regular feedback allows for timely interventions when issues arise. PIPs ensure transparency, giving employees a fair chance to address challenges before termination becomes necessary.

- By incorporating these consistent check-ins and feedback loops, recognition becomes part of the organization's daily rhythm, making it more sustainable and effective.

LAW FIRM CASE STUDY: O'MELVENY & MYERS LLP

In the legal industry, recognition can often be limited by a focus on billable hours. O'Melveny & Myers LLP faced similar challenges, where the emphasis on hours worked led to feelings of undervaluation among support staff and junior associates. To address this issue, the firm broadened its recognition criteria to include contributions to firm culture, mentorship, and community service, moving beyond traditional measures like billable hours.

The firm implemented a peer recognition platform, allowing employees to nominate colleagues for their efforts. This shift made it possible for all employees to be acknowledged, regardless of their roles. As a result, O'Melveny & Myers experienced improved morale and retention rates, particularly among junior staff, who felt that their contributions were finally valued.[23] By broadening its recognition focus, the firm fostered a more inclusive work environment that positively impacted engagement and morale across the organization.

This example highlights how expanding recognition criteria to encompass a wider range of employee contributions can benefit even traditionally rigid environments.

PROGRESS OVER PERFECTION IN RECOGNITION PROGRAMS

When I worked with a real estate development company, implementing a performance management system was initially met with resistance. Leaders felt overwhelmed by the time required to complete performance reviews, finding the process cumbersome. We simplified the reviews to include just a few key questions—what went well, challenges faced, goals for the next year, and feedback for the manager. This focused approach made conversations more productive, evolving to include company values like teamwork, further reinforcing a culture of recognition.

---

23   "O'Melveny Ranked among Top Three 'Best Law Firms to Work for' by Vault for Unprecedented Ninth Consecutive Year," O'Melveny, accessed November 4, 2024, https://www.omm.com/news/awards-honors/o-melveny-ranked-among-top-three-best-law-firms-to-work-for-by-vault-for-unprecedented-ninth-consecutive-year/.

Similarly, when I connected with a partner at a law firm, I found that there was no structured performance assessment system. Success was measured by whether the business made enough to cover overhead. However, after we discussed how recognition and development go hand in hand, the partner recognized the value of implementing regular performance reviews and professional development conversations. These reviews became more than just a means to acknowledge achievements—they became a platform for developing leaders within the company, driving motivation and long-term growth. Employees had been eager for feedback, and providing it fostered a sense of ownership in the company's success.

The lesson here is clear: perfection is often the enemy of progress. Start simple, prioritize consistent recognition and feedback, and refine processes over time. The most successful recognition programs evolve by beginning with achievable steps that build momentum and create lasting cultural change.

RECOGNITION AS A PATH TO LEADERSHIP DEVELOPMENT

Recognition is not just about celebrating success—it's about creating a clear pathway for employees to grow into leadership roles. A survey of 1,500 business professionals revealed that employees who feel heard are 4.6 times more likely to perform to the best of their abilities.[24] Effective communication also enhances productivity by 25 percent, while a lack of communication is cited as the root cause of workplace failures by 86 percent of employees.

I once suggested to a CEO that, when promoting an employee, they send an email to the entire team explaining why the promotion was made, highlighting the values and strengths that led to this decision. This not only serves as recognition for the promoted employee but also communicates the qualities valued by the organization, making leadership qualities more visible and aspirational for others.

TRANSITION TO LEADERSHIP AND GROWTH

Recognition is more than a motivational tool; it sets the foundation for leadership. Consistent acknowledgment cultivates individual strengths, while clear communication ensures employees understand what is valued by the company. This alignment empowers leadership and drives growth— topics we'll explore further in "Chapter 5: Empowering Leadership and Growth."

In the next chapter, we will dive into how reinforcing a company's purpose, mission, vision, and values inspires employees to grow, take initiative, and

---

24   Naz Beheshti, "10 Timely Statistics about the Connection between Employee Engagement and Wellness," Forbes, February 20, 2024, https://www. forbes.com/sites/nazbeheshti/2019/01/16/10-timely-statistics-about-the-connection-between-employee-engagement-and-wellness/.

lead. By building a culture of recognition, you not only motivate employees today—but also lay the groundwork for a future where empowered leaders drive the company forward.

CONCLUSION: CULTURE OF RECOGNITION

In this chapter, we've seen how a culture of recognition is essential not only for motivating employees but also for building a strong, cohesive organization where individuals feel valued and driven to contribute their best. Recognition is more than a reward; it's a means of cultivating trust, fostering engagement, and aligning employees with the company's vision. By making recognition an integral part of your company's rhythm—from one-on-one check-ins to structured reviews—you create an environment where every contribution is acknowledged, reinforcing a sense of belonging and purpose.

The examples we discussed, from formal recognition platforms to simple, intentional feedback, illustrate how companies can transform morale and engagement by embedding consistent, meaningful acknowledgment into everyday operations. The lesson is clear: a recognition program doesn't have to be perfect to be impactful. Start with achievable steps, and let the culture evolve with time, reinforcing values and promoting a shared commitment to success.

Recognition is not only a tool for motivation but also a pathway to growth and leadership development. By celebrating strengths and communicating the values that matter most, you create a framework where future leaders feel inspired and empowered to rise. As we transition into the next chapter, "Empowering Leadership and Growth," we'll explore how reinforcing purpose, mission, vision, and values further ignites employees' potential, setting the stage for a culture where empowered leaders drive the company forward.

KEY TAKEAWAYS

- **Recognition Drives Engagement:** Studies show that regular recognition increases productivity, profitability, and employee retention, proving that appreciation is key to employee commitment.

- **Structured Programs Work:** Minto Group and O'Melveny & Myers illustrate how formal recognition systems improve morale, connection, and retention.

- **Recognition Builds Leadership:** Regular acknowledgment provides a blueprint for leadership, helping employees understand what is valued and motivating them to grow.

- **Consistency Over Perfection:** Begin with simple recognition initiatives that are easy to implement and refine over time to ensure progress and long-term impact.

- **Recognition Enhances Communication:** By embedding recognition into everyday interactions, companies not only create a more positive environment but also strengthen trust and team cohesion.

ACTION STEPS

- **Implement a Recognition Platform:** Consider tools like Bonusly, Workhuman, or Kudos to establish a formal recognition program that enables peer-to-peer acknowledgment and real-time feedback.

- **Broaden Recognition Criteria:** Expand beyond performance metrics to include contributions to company culture, mentorship, and community involvement.

- **Establish Regular Review Cycles:** Integrate recognition into weekly one-on-ones, mid-year reviews, and annual evaluations, focusing on both achievements and growth opportunities.

- **Start Simple:** Begin with a few key questions in performance reviews and refine the process as it evolves, favoring consistency over complexity.

- **Promote Recognition in Leadership:** Ensure that leaders actively participate in recognizing employee efforts and communicate the qualities valued within the organization.

Creating a culture of recognition is not merely about acknowledging achievements—it's about building trust, fostering communication, and empowering employees to grow into future leaders. Recognition sets a clear path for development, helps align individual contributions with the company's mission, and lays the foundation for long-term success. By implementing structured yet simple recognition processes, organizations can enhance engagement, motivation, and retention while also supporting leadership development.

Chapter 5

Empowering Leadership and Growth

"Our mission statement about treating people with respect and dignity is not just words but a creed we live by every day. You can't expect your employees to exceed the expectations of your customers if you don't exceed the employees' expectations of management."

—HOWARD SCHULTZ

Leadership is a journey fueled by personal and professional growth, and it thrives when employees feel connected to the company's core values. When individuals understand the organization's purpose, mission, and vision, they are empowered to take on leadership roles that align with both their personal aspirations and the company's goals.

THE POWER OF PURPOSE, MISSION, VISION AND VALUES

At the heart of every empowered leader is a deep connection to purpose. Purpose gives employees a reason to show up every day, and when that purpose aligns with the company's mission, it drives engagement, motivation, and growth. Leaders are born when they can link their day-to-day tasks with a greater organizational purpose.

In my recruitment experience, one of the first things candidates ask about is the company's culture, which is often a reflection of the company's mission, purpose, and values. People want to feel that they belong to an organization that aligns with their values and goals. A McKinsey study found that 70 percent of professionals view work as a key component of their purpose.[25] Companies that can clearly communicate their purpose attract top talent and inspire their employees to perform at their best because they feel like they are part of something bigger.

Employees also want to work in a culture that matches their authentic selves. Since the COVID-19 pandemic,

---

25   Naina Dhingra and Bill Schaninger, "The Search for Purpose at Work," McKinsey & Company, June 3, 2021, https://www.mckinsey.com/capabilities/people-and-organizational-performance/our-insights/the-search-for-purpose-at-work.

the lines between personal and professional life have blurred, with hybrid work models, remote work, and a greater emphasis on work-life balance. Employees now want to feel that their work is an extension of who they are. I recall one Gen Z candidate who turned down an offer because he said it would "kill his soul." This speaks to how strongly younger generations, in particular, value purpose and alignment with their work.

CRAFTING A MISSION THAT INSPIRES GROWTH

Your company's mission is a powerful tool that should inspire employees to grow into leadership roles. A well-crafted mission defines your target audience, explains the contribution your company makes, and highlights what sets you apart from competitors. Here's a breakdown of how to develop a mission that empowers.

- **The Key Market**: Who is your audience? (e.g., Small business owners.)

- **Your Contribution**: What impact does your business make? (e.g., Helping business leaders save time, increase profitability, and improve employee retention.)

- **Distinction**: What makes your business unique? (e.g., Specialized skills, experience, passion for change.)

A powerful mission statement clarifies the company's direction and gives employees a roadmap for how they can contribute to the bigger picture.

For example, at Marriott International, a company that began as a small root beer stand and grew into a Fortune 200 business, leadership remained committed to its core mission: "If we take care of our people, they will take care of our customers, and the customers will come back."[26] This consistent, values-driven mission empowered leaders at every level to grow the company while maintaining a people-first culture.

ALIGNING LEADERSHIP WITH CORE VALUES

Once the mission is clear, the next step is to ensure that leadership reflects the company's values. Authentic leadership is rooted in consistency, and when employees see leaders embodying the company's values, it builds trust. For example, a construction client of mine prominently displayed their values in their conference room, so both employees and visitors were reminded of the guiding principles that shaped the company's culture. This kind of visibility helps employees align their actions with the company's values and strengthens the overall culture.

---

26   "Our Story," Our Story, accessed November 4, 2024, https://www.marriott.com/about/culture-and-values/history.mi?msockid=289a069a51096f-cf3c3415ee50336eb0.

I worked with a law firm partner who struggled to establish leadership behaviors aligned with his firm's mission. His primary focus was on profitability, but there was no framework for measuring success or supporting the professional development of his team. Once we introduced performance reviews that were aligned with the company's values, not only did the team become more engaged, but the leaders also began to develop the next generation of leadership within the firm.

In the recruitment process, it's important to ask candidates about their alignment with the company's values. Asking questions like "How did you contribute to your previous team's success?" helps assess if a potential leader shares the same values as your company. Aligning new hires with the company's mission and values from the start sets the stage for their growth into leadership roles.

DEVELOPING LEADERSHIP THROUGH AUTHENTICITY

Leadership is built on trust, and trust comes from authenticity. People want to follow genuine leaders who consistently live the values they espouse. As I've observed throughout my career, authenticity isn't about perfection—it's about showing up as your true self and inspiring others to do the same.

The importance of authenticity among leaders is highlighted through recent populist political movements throughout the world, particularly in the United States. Donald Trump's unlikely rise to the US presidency was characterized by a certain unfiltered communication style that deviated so far from that of traditional politicians that what might have otherwise historically been a liability became an asset among a significant number of voters. His shedding of the norms of political civility fostered the perception that he was a no-nonsense, tell-it-like-it-is non-politician: in a word, authentic. Whether real or merely perceived, the authenticity attributed to President Trump was critical in amassing loyal supporters, who overlooked or forgave behaviors and statements that may have been serious roadblocks for a traditional politician.

This is because his verbose and non-traditional speech gives President Trump's supporters the opportunity to cite often the fact that "he tells it how it is" as a quality that helped win them over. This led many to view him as an authentic truth-teller. Authenticity was a key reason Donald Trump resonated with voters during his presidential campaign. While opinions on his policies varied widely, his straightforward, unscripted style appealed to people who valued authenticity. This example shows how authenticity can create a strong connection between leaders and their followers. Similarly, when leaders in a company show up authentically, it fosters trust and encourages employees to follow suit, creating a culture where people feel safe to grow.

THE ROLE OF LEADERSHIP IN EMPOWERING TEAMS

Empowering leadership means giving teams clear direction while fostering independence and growth. Leaders must know how to delegate, guide, and support their teams so that everyone is rowing in the same direction. When the entire team is aligned with the company's mission and values, it becomes easier to achieve shared goals.

For instance, when leaders focus on building the next generation of talent, they create an environment where employees are encouraged to step into leadership roles. This requires mentorship, support, and providing opportunities for growth. The best leaders know that their success is measured not just by their own accomplishments but by how well they prepare others to lead.

Empowering leadership is also about giving employees a sense of ownership. When people feel that their contributions matter and that they're making a real impact, they are motivated to perform at their best. This sense of ownership and engagement leads to increased productivity, innovation, and long-term growth.

CONCLUSION: TRANSITION TO BUILDING TRUST AND CONNECTION

In this chapter, we've examined how empowering leadership goes hand-in-hand with authenticity, alignment, and a commitment to fostering growth. True leadership is not simply about overseeing tasks but inspiring others to connect with a shared mission, cultivate their strengths, and feel deeply valued within the organization. When leaders embody the company's purpose, mission, vision, and values, they create an environment where employees feel motivated, trusted, and engaged to contribute their best.

At the heart of empowering leadership is a dedication to authenticity and connection. By showing up as genuine and transparent, leaders foster a culture where people feel safe to innovate, grow, and work toward common goals. This trust encourages a sense of ownership and pride among employees, which in turn drives performance, loyalty, and long-term success.

As you continue your leadership journey, remember that empowering others is an investment in your company's future. It's about nurturing talent that will not only meet today's goals but also champion your organization's values and vision well into the future.

In the next chapter, "Building Trust and Connection Through Branding Strategy," we'll explore how to strengthen these connections further by aligning your external brand with your internal culture. By creating an authentic and consistent brand strategy, you'll reinforce trust with your team and communicate a compelling message that resonates both within and beyond the company.

KEY TAKEAWAYS

- **Purpose Drives Engagement:** When employees connect their work to a meaningful purpose, they are more engaged, motivated, and committed to the organization's success.

- **Authentic Leadership Builds Trust:** Leaders who show up as genuine and transparent foster a culture of trust where employees feel safe to contribute, innovate, and grow.

- **Values Should Guide Leadership:** Leadership that aligns with core values reinforces a cohesive culture, establishing consistency and trust across the organization.

- **Empowerment Fuels Growth:** Empowering employees with autonomy and ownership motivates them to perform at their best and prepares them for future leadership roles within the company.

- **Leadership Development Is a Strategic Investment:** Developing future leaders through mentorship and growth opportunities ensures the sustainability of the company's culture and vision, preparing it for long-term success.

ACTION STEPS

- **Define and Reinforce Purpose, Mission, and Values:** Clearly communicate the company's purpose, mission, and values across all levels, ensuring that employees understand how their work aligns with the organization's goals.

- **Model Authentic Leadership:** Encourage leaders to be transparent and genuine, setting an example that fosters trust and encourages employees to bring their full selves to work.

- **Empower Employees with Ownership:** Give employees the autonomy to make decisions and take ownership of their projects, enhancing engagement and a sense of responsibility.

- **Recognize Value-Aligned Contributions:** Publicly acknowledge employees who exemplify company values, reinforcing what matters most to the organization and inspiring others.

- **Invest in Leadership Development:** Create pathways for growth by offering mentorship, training, or project leadership opportunities that prepare high-potential employees for future leadership roles.

As we move from leadership and growth to building trust and connection, it's crucial to recognize that leadership cannot thrive without trust. Leadership is about inspiring people to follow, but for that to happen, leaders must cultivate solid and authentic connections with their teams. This is where branding strategy plays a key role—not just in how the company presents itself to the outside world but in how it fosters trust and pride within the organization.

In "Chapter 6: Building Trust and Connection Through Branding Strategy," we'll explore how branding strategy can strengthen trust and create deeper connections, both internally among employees and externally with customers. A strong brand not only defines the company's reputation but also aligns the team with the company's mission, reinforcing a sense of pride and engagement.

Chapter 6

Building Trust and Connection Through Branding Strategy

"To win in the marketplace, you must first win in the workplace."

—DOUG CONANT

In today's hyper-connected world, your brand is more than just a logo or a catchy slogan—it's the living, breathing essence of your company. It's how people perceive you, how they talk about you, and how they experience your company. When employees are part of the branding process, it builds pride and fosters trust within your team. But even more importantly, it creates a lasting connection with your customers, candidates, and community.

THE POWER OF A STRONG BRAND FOR EMPLOYEES

When employees are connected to the brand and understand how they represent the company, they feel more engaged, more loyal, and more motivated. A clear and inspiring brand creates a shared identity among employees, giving them a sense of belonging and pride in the company's mission.

At one company I worked with, bad reviews on Glassdoor became a serious issue. Candidates stopped showing up for interviews, and job offers were being declined at an alarming rate. The online reputation was making it nearly impossible to attract top talent. And trust me, news travels fast—especially online. In fact, a 2021 Glassdoor study found that 86 percent of employees and job seekers research company reviews and ratings before deciding where to apply for a job.[27] If people perceive your company poorly online, it can tank your recruitment efforts, and top performers will run for the hills.

However, the opposite is also true. When employees feel proud of the brand they represent, they become ambassadors for the company. They spread the word, refer great talent to the company, and share their positive experiences. I spoke with a rapidly growing law firm in Phoenix that mentioned their best hires

---

27   Glassdoor Team, The most important employer branding statistics to know - glassdoor for employers, April 5, 2021, https://www.glassdoor.com/employers/blog/most-important-employer-branding-statistics/.

consistently came from referrals—employees who loved working there wanted their friends and family to join the team.

BUILDING AN ONLINE PRESENCE TO ATTRACT AND RETAIN TALENT

In today's job market, having an online presence is crucial. LinkedIn, Facebook, Instagram, and Glassdoor are all part of the modern talent pipeline. Companies with strong social media strategies have a far easier time attracting top performers, and those who actively engage with their communities are more likely to retain them. In 2021, Edelman's Trust Barometer report found that 68 percent of people believe it's more important to trust the brands they buy or work for today than it was in the past.[28]

Here's a tip: don't just focus on what your company does. Tell the story of *who* you are and why people should want to work with you. Highlight your company's mission, values, and purpose across social platforms. A well-rounded brand strategy involves your employees, shows them how they fit into the bigger picture, and reinforces their importance to the company.

And remember—it's not just about getting noticed. It's about building trust. According to the Edelman

---

28   Anna-Lena Schildt, "Edelman Trust Barometer 2021," Edelman Deutschland, February 16, 2021, https://www.edelman.de/en/research/edelman-trust-barometer-2021.

report, trust drives growth.[29] Trust isn't built by great marketing alone—it's reinforced by actions that align with the brand message. As Patrick Lencioni points out in *The Five Dysfunctions of a Team*, building a foundation of trust is critical for high-performing teams.[30]

HOW A NEGATIVE BRAND EXPERIENCE CAN IMPACT HIRING

I once worked with a candidate who seemed genuinely excited about a job opportunity. She had an engaging phone screen and asked all the right questions. But after speaking with her network and checking out the company's online reputation, she decided not to move forward. The company had a low rating on Yelp—just three out of five stars. Although there were some positive reviews, a recent business setback led to negative press and a series of unfavorable comments. Despite changes in leadership, the damage had been done, and the company's reputation continued to suffer.

For companies facing similar challenges, my advice is to focus on rebuilding trust, both online and internally. Start by encouraging satisfied customers, clients, and employees to share their positive experiences through reviews. Consider implementing tools like

29   Daniel J. Edelman Holdings, "2023 Global Citizenship Report | Edelman," Edelman, 2023, https://citizenship.edelman.com/2023/home.
30   Patrick Lencioni, *The Five Dysfunctions of a Team: Team Assessment* (San Francisco, Calif: Pfeiffer, a Wiley Imprint, 2012).

Net Promoter Score (NPS) surveys to gather valuable feedback and consistently follow up on both positive and negative reviews. A brand strategy cannot simply exist on paper—it must be demonstrated through actions that restore and build trust.

Even with negative reviews, it's essential to respond publicly. When people see that a company is actively addressing concerns, it demonstrates transparency and a commitment to problem-solving. A constructive response can help offset negative impressions and show potential candidates and clients that the company values feedback and is committed to improvement.

CREATING A BRAND EMPLOYEES CAN BE PROUD TO BE A PART OF

A company's brand goes far beyond a slick website or a trendy office space. It's built layer by layer, starting with internal communication and extending outward to your customers, candidates, and community. Here are some steps to help strengthen your brand and foster connection.

- **Start with Your Website**: Make sure your mission, values, and culture are front and center. Use this as an opportunity to showcase what makes your company unique.

- **Leverage Social Media**: Share stories about your employees, celebrate milestones, and highlight your company's achievements. This is not just for customers—it's also for current and potential employees.

- **Respond to Online Reviews**: Whether they're positive or negative, engage with your audience. Be proactive in addressing concerns, especially if leadership has changed or the company has evolved.

- **Encourage Employee Testimonials**: A video of employees sharing their journey and why they love working at your company can be a powerful tool. It humanizes the brand and shows that people matter.

- **Get Referrals from Your Top Performers**: Your best employees likely know others who would be a great fit. When employees refer their friends or people in their network, they're helping to build a sense of community and connection.

When you invest in your brand, it's not just about attracting customers—it's about creating an environment where employees feel valued and want to stay.

CONCLUSION: THE LINK BETWEEN BRANDING AND RETENTION

In this chapter, we've explored the critical role of branding in building trust and connection, emphasizing that a strong brand extends far beyond external appearances. When employees feel aligned with the company's brand and mission, they become powerful advocates, attracting like-minded talent and fostering a culture of pride and loyalty. A positive brand presence, both online and internally, builds the foundation for a thriving organization where people are motivated to contribute and grow.

Effective branding is not just about attracting talent; it's about creating a lasting connection that engages employees and reinforces the values they experience day to day. By prioritizing transparency, authenticity, and responsiveness, your brand becomes a beacon of trust, drawing in candidates who resonate with your culture and inspiring employees to represent your company with pride.

In the next section, we'll dive into strategies for retaining and integrating this valuable talent. Through effective onboarding, continuous development, and a supportive work environment, we'll explore how to cultivate a workplace where employees are engaged, empowered, and ready to drive your organization forward for the long term.

KEY TAKEAWAYS

- **Branding Is a Core Component of Trust and Retention:** A strong brand doesn't just attract talent; it fosters loyalty, pride, and long-term connection among employees who feel aligned with the company's mission and values.

- **Employees as Brand Ambassadors:** When employees feel connected to the brand, they naturally become ambassadors, sharing positive experiences that can enhance recruitment and retention.

- **Online Reputation Matters:** Potential hires frequently check online reviews and ratings before applying. A positive online presence is essential to attract and retain top talent, while negative reviews can deter candidates.

- **Transparency and Responsiveness Build Trust:** Addressing feedback, both positive and negative, publicly and constructively reinforces trust, showing that your company values and listens to its employees and customers.

- **Storytelling Is Key in Branding:** An effective brand strategy shares the company's mission, values, and unique story, helping employees and candidates see where they fit in and why they should want to be a part of it.

ACTION STEPS

- **Strengthen Your Online Presence:** Regularly update your website and social media channels to reflect your company's mission, values, and culture. Use these platforms to share employee stories, company milestones, and achievements.

- **Encourage and Manage Online Reviews:** Invite satisfied employees, clients, and customers to leave reviews on platforms like Glassdoor and Yelp. Address both positive and negative reviews publicly to show your commitment to feedback and improvement.

- **Engage Employees in Branding Initiatives:** Involve employees in creating brand content, such as testimonials, videos, or social media takeovers, to make them feel more connected to the brand and proud to represent it.

- **Promote Your Brand Internally and Externally:** Ensure your mission, values, and company culture are visible in the workplace through signage, team meetings, and digital communication. Externally, highlight these same qualities to align public perception with internal culture.

- **Leverage Employee Referrals:** Encourage top employees to refer like-minded talent. Offer a structured referral program to incentivize employees and create a sense of community and connection within your workforce.

Retaining great talent goes beyond keeping people on payroll—it's about creating an environment where employees feel genuinely fulfilled and see a future with your organization. In this section, we'll focus on building that long-term commitment by ensuring employees feel a deep sense of belonging, purpose, and growth within your company. Starting with a seamless onboarding and integration process, followed by ongoing development and clear career pathing, and culminating in a positive work environment, each chapter provides actionable insights for nurturing satisfaction and loyalty. Together, these elements will help you create a workplace that not only retains talent but inspires them to invest their best in your organization's future.

OVERVIEW OF PART 3: RETAIN (FOCUS: LONG-TERM COMMITMENT AND SATISFACTION)

- **Chapter 7: Effective Onboarding and Integration**

  - Ensuring a smooth transition and a positive initial experience to encourage retention from the start.

- **Chapter 8: Continuous Employee Development and Career Pathing**

  - Offering clear growth paths and development opportunities to retain employees in the long run.

- **Chapter 9: Building a Positive Work Environment and Engagement**

  - Cultivating a work environment that promotes well-being, loyalty, and work-life balance to keep employees satisfied and committed over time.

As we transition from inspire to retain, it's important to remember that a strong brand not only attracts top talent but also helps keep them. Employees who are proud of where they work and who feel connected to the mission and values are far more likely to stay with the company for the long haul. This sense of connection fosters loyalty and encourages employees to become advocates for the brand.

In the next section, we'll dive into how onboarding, employee development, and ongoing engagement play key roles in retaining the talent you've worked so hard to attract. We'll explore strategies to ensure employees feel supported from day one and how cultivating a strong retention strategy can drive long-term success for your company.

PART 3

Retain

Focus: Long-Term Commitment and Satisfaction

"Always treat your employees exactly as you want them to treat your best customers."

—STEPHEN R. COVEY

Retention is the art of turning a workplace into a destination—a place where employees not only contribute but also flourish. It's not just about keeping your people; it's about creating an ecosystem where they can grow, innovate, and thrive alongside the organization.

Retention isn't transactional; it's relational. It's about recognizing the shared journey between the employer and the employee—a journey built on trust, mutual investment, and a shared vision for the future. When done well, retention transforms an organization into a resilient, adaptable community capable of weathering challenges and seizing opportunities.

While much of the conversation around retention focuses on preventing turnover, this section challenges you to think about retention as a *two-way partnership*. Employees stay because they choose to, not because they feel trapped or obligated. What would happen if organizations stopped asking, *"How do we keep employees from leaving?"* and started asking, *"How do we make them want to stay?"*

In this section, we'll provide fresh insights, actionable tools, and real-world examples to help you create a retention strategy that goes beyond metrics. It's time to think of retention not as the final step but as the ultimate investment in the long-term success of your people and your organization.

Chapter 7

Effective Onboarding and Integration

*Treat employees like they make
a difference, and they will."*

—JIM GOODNIGHT

Onboarding is one of the most important, yet often overlooked, processes in talent management. First impressions matter, and for new hires, the onboarding experience sets the tone for their entire journey with your company. It's not just about filling out paperwork or watching a few training videos—it's about integrating new employees into your culture, building relationships, and setting them up for success.

THE TURNOVER PROBLEM AND THE
POWER OF ONBOARDING

At one of my previous companies, we were hiring rapidly, and at first, things seemed to be going smoothly—well, as smoothly as they can when you are hiring over 100 people in one with an HR party of one. The company had grown from ten people in the headquarters to now multiple people in the office, plus having locations throughout Phoenix for apartments where employees working in property management and construction as the five different complexes were being renovated.

Also, there were properties acquired in Michigan and Oklahoma, which meant there were employees in both of those states who also needed to understand the core roots and what was being done in Phoenix to be consistent with the company values, mission, and vision across the nation and with clients. After evaluating the past year's performance to review people who had left the company, it became clear that some managers had higher turnover rates than others. Luckily, we were conducting exit interviews to gain feedback, which consistently highlighted a lack of connection and clarity during the first few months as key reasons for leaving. This made a lot of sense because managers were sometimes onboarded with employees who would work for them, which meant they were learning together but not necessarily aware of the standard operating procedures (SOP) for specific tasks.

The solution? A robust onboarding program that didn't just get people in the door but set them up for long-term success. This meant having the right tools, knowing who to connect with when challenges arise, where to find documents and SOPs, having more training from subject matter experts (SME) on different software, and learning from the beginning the right way to handle clients and business concerns.

Our first goal was to reduce the ninety-day turnover rate. We built an onboarding program that focused on collaboration, clear communication, and creating an environment where new hires felt part of the team from day one. A sense of belonging, safety, and certainty are key pieces that allow an employee to feel connected to the company. It wasn't just about making sure they had their login credentials or knew where the coffee machine was; we wanted them to understand the company's mission, values, and the faces behind the titles.

I once heard about a new hire who asked a random colleague what his role was, only to find out that he was speaking with the COO. Oops! This highlighted a gap in our onboarding process. We quickly adjusted by including leadership introductions in the first few weeks. This helped new hires get familiar not just with names but with faces and gave them a sense of connection with company leadership. We even went a step further and would have the C-suite come in during the onboarding to introduce themselves and share something about themselves and even the company.

For example, the CEO would end the onboarding with profit and loss. He would help people understand different costs in the business, especially on the property side, to see how one employee could contribute to the bottom line, save money, and make a considerable contribution over time. It was a valuable lesson that created the foundation for what was expected. It also created the dynamic that the CEO was reachable; he was relatable, and he was someone that people could respect and admire because he took time out of his busy schedule to meet the new people on the team.

Once the onboarding program was launched, we saw a massive improvement in the 90-day numbers. We achieved an 80 percent retention rate in the first six months after implementing the change.

A SAMPLE FIRST-WEEK AGENDA

Here's a sample of a structured, engaging first week. It should give new hires a sense of certainty, build relationships, and set clear expectations for their role and integration into the company.

Day 1: Orientation and Relationship Building

- **9:00 a.m. – 10:30 a.m.: Welcome and Orientation**

  - Introduce company culture, mission, history, and key milestones.

  - Share the company's vision for the future and how the new hire's role contributes.

- **10:30 a.m. – 11:00 a.m.: Office Tour and IT Setup**

  - Walk through the office or virtual tools.

  - Resolve any IT issues and collect necessary compliance documents.

- **11:00 a.m. – 12:00 p.m.: Team and Stakeholder Introductions**

  - Team members share their roles and responsibilities.

  - Include a short icebreaker to foster connection.

- **12:00 p.m. – 1:00 p.m.: Lunch with Manager or Team**

  - Build rapport in a casual, friendly setting.

- **1:00 p.m. – 4:00 p.m.: HR Overview and Ongoing Projects**

  - Review company policies, benefits, and key projects.

- Add the new hire to upcoming team meetings and project updates.

- **4:00 p.m. – 5:00 p.m.: One-on-One Check-In with Supervisor**

    - Set expectations for the first week, 30, 60, and 90 days.

    - Align on immediate goals and discuss how success will be measured.

Day 2: Training and Hands-On Learning

- **9:00 a.m. – 10:30 a.m.: Software Training**

    - Introduce key tools and assign a peer mentor for guidance.

- **10:30 a.m. – 12:00 p.m.: Shadowing Team Members**

    - Observe processes, followed by hands-on practice with real-time feedback.

- **12:00 p.m. – 1:00 p.m.: Lunch with Peer Mentor**

    - Discuss best practices and ask informal questions about the role.

- **1:00 p.m. – 4:30 p.m.: Repetition and Skill Practice**

    - Allow time for independent work to build confidence.

o   Provide support through periodic check-ins
and feedback.

Day 3: Deeper Integration and Networking

- **9:00 a.m. – 12:00 p.m.: Job-Specific Tasks**

    o   Dive deeper into role responsibilities and
    practice with supervision.

- **12:00 p.m. – 1:00 p.m.: Lunch with Cross-
Department Colleagues**

    o   Foster cross-functional collaboration and
    understanding.

- **1:00 p.m. – 5:00 p.m.: Hands-On Work and
Feedback Session**

    o   Provide additional practice time, then gather
    feedback on the onboarding experience.

This structure integrates **learning, relationship-
building, and feedback loops** into the first week,
creating a supportive and engaging onboarding
experience. By focusing on repetition, team
connections, and alignment with the company's
vision, you set the stage for long-term retention.

THE COST OF POOR ONBOARDING

We often think of onboarding as a one-and-done
process, but the truth is that it's an ongoing investment

that pays off in the long run. Let's look at some stats that show the real impact of onboarding.[31]

- **Forty-three percent of employees** report receiving no more than a one-day orientation. Short, disorganized onboarding processes create uncertainty and confusion.

- **Twelve percent of employees** say their organization has a good onboarding process. That's a shockingly low number. Imagine the retention and engagement benefits if more companies took onboarding seriously.

- **Twenty percent of employees** quit within the first 45 days. This is due primarily to poor onboarding experiences that fail to set clear expectations or provide adequate support.

- **Sixty-nine percent of employees** are more likely to stay with a company for three years if they've experienced a well-structured onboarding process.

When onboarding is done right, it shows new hires that the company is invested in their success. This, in turn, makes them more likely to invest in the company. In contrast, poor onboarding sends the message that the company is disorganized or

---

31   Solveig Rundquist, "33 Employee Training Statistics and Trends to Level up in 2024," Mentimeter, June 4, 2024, https://www.mentimeter.com/blog/training/employee-training-statistics.

indifferent, pushing employees to look for better opportunities elsewhere.

BUILDING RELATIONSHIPS THROUGH ONBOARDING

One key benefit of a strong onboarding program is the opportunity to build relationships across departments. When employees are siloed, they often blame other teams when things go wrong. However, when you foster connections early on, employees are more likely to collaborate and communicate effectively. They'll be more empathetic when issues arise, knowing the person on the other side of that email or Slack message.

At our company, we made it a point to introduce new hires to different teams early on. We even implemented lunch sessions where employees from different departments could meet informally. This small effort created an environment where employees felt more connected and less intimidated when reaching out for help.

ONBOARDING ACROSS REMOTE AND HYBRID TEAMS

Remote work has added new layers of complexity to the onboarding process. According to a study, 63 percent of remote employees are more likely to leave their employer than in-office workers.[32] Why? Because it's harder to feel connected and engaged when you're physically distant from your team. That's why creating a robust virtual onboarding process is crucial.

At one point, our company experimented with virtual and in-person onboarding sessions. We found that a combination of the two worked best, allowing flexibility for remote workers while still fostering a sense of community. We held virtual check-ins, used tools like Slack and Zoom for communication, and made sure that every new hire, whether remote or on-site, felt included and supported.

THE CEO'S PERSPECTIVE

One of the most impactful moments during our onboarding process was when the CEO would come in and talk about ROI, profit, and loss. Sharing the company's financials gave new hires a sense of ownership. It showed them how their role contributed to the company's success and gave them a clearer understanding of the bigger picture. When employees feel like they're part of something meaningful, they're more likely to stay engaged and perform at a higher level.

---

32   Roy Maurer, "Rethinking Onboarding for the Remote-Work Era," Welcome to SHRM, December 21, 2023, https://www.shrm.org/topics-tools/news/hr-magazine/rethinking-onboarding-remote-work-era.

The onboarding process is your first chance to create a culture of ownership and accountability. By showing new hires how their work contributes to the company's success, you motivate them to excel. It's not just about training them for their role—it's about inspiring them to take pride in it.

TYING ONBOARDING TO RETENTION AND GROWTH

Onboarding is more than just a check-the-box process; it's your first real chance to build a foundation of trust, engagement, and clarity for your new hires. Done well, it can have a lasting impact. In fact, businesses that implement a smooth, structured onboarding process see a 52 percent higher retention rate than those that don't.[33] When you invest in a strong onboarding program, you not only reduce turnover but also set the stage for long-term success, both for the employee and the company. A well-thought-out onboarding process creates alignment between the company's mission and values and the individual's role within the organization, leading to a more profound sense of purpose and belonging.

However, onboarding is only the first step in the employee's journey. While it sets the tone, what comes next is equally important in maintaining that

---

33   Oak Engage, "24 Shocking Employee Onboarding Statistics in 2023 - Oak Engage," Oak Digital Workplace, July 23, 2024, https://www.oak.com/blog/employee-onboarding-statistics/.

engagement, fostering growth, and ensuring that employees see a future with your company.

CONCLUSION: KEEPING THE MOMENTUM GOING

Onboarding is not just a process—it's the foundation upon which the entire employee experience is built. It's the first impression that determines whether a new hire feels like an integral part of the team or a disconnected cog in the machine. When done well, onboarding sets the stage for trust, engagement, and long-term success.

As we've explored in this chapter, effective onboarding is about more than logistics. It's about creating a meaningful connection between the new hire and the company's mission, values, and culture. It's about equipping employees with the tools, knowledge, and relationships they need to thrive.

Your onboarding program reflects your company's priorities and culture. By focusing on clarity, connection, and continuous improvement, you can create a welcoming experience that resonates with employees long after their first week.

Remember, onboarding is your chance to show new hires they're more than just employees—they're partners in your company's mission. When you treat onboarding as a vital part of the employee journey, you're not just filling seats; you're building a team that's aligned, engaged, and ready to drive your organization forward.

KEY TAKEAWAYS

- **Clarity and Connection Matter**: Set clear expectations, provide role-specific training, and foster relationships that make employees feel valued and supported.

- **Leadership Involvement Counts**: When leaders engage in the onboarding process, it humanizes the organization and builds trust.

- **Structure Breeds Success**: A well-organized onboarding program increases retention, reduces uncertainty, and ensures new hires hit the ground running.

- **Onboarding Never Stops**: It's not a one-day event but an ongoing investment in your team's growth and satisfaction.

- **Belonging Drives Retention**: A sense of belonging created early through team connections and shared values increases engagement and reduces turnover.

- **Customization Enhances Impact**: Tailoring the onboarding experience to individual roles and learning styles ensures new hires feel seen and supported from the start.

- **Cross-Department Collaboration Matters**: Early exposure to other teams fosters understanding, reduces silos, and encourages a culture of collaboration.

- **Feedback Is a Two-Way Street**: Onboarding is an opportunity for new hires to share their initial impressions, helping you improve the process while reinforcing that their voice matters.

- **Mentorship Accelerates Success**: Assigning peer mentors during onboarding helps new hires navigate challenges, build relationships, and feel part of the team more quickly.

- **The Power of First Impressions**: A well-executed onboarding program sends a strong message about your company's values, professionalism, and commitment to its people, setting the tone for long-term success.

ACTION STEPS

- **Create a Detailed First-Week Agenda:** Design an agenda that balances learning, relationship-building, and hands-on work. Include specific times for orientation, training, team introductions, and leadership interaction. Share the agenda with the new hire before their first day to provide clarity and reduce anxiety.

- **Develop a Comprehensive Onboarding Deck:** Include key elements such as:

  ○ **Mission, Vision, and Values**: Explain the company's "why" and how employees contribute to it.

  ○ **Company History**: Share milestones and stories that connect the new hire to the organization's journey.

  ○ **Leadership Introductions**: Include photos, bios, and roles of leadership to humanize them and foster accessibility. Ensure the deck is visually engaging and easy to understand, serving as a reusable tool for future hires.

- **Integrate Leadership into Onboarding:** Schedule time for senior leaders to meet with new hires, whether in person or virtually. Encourage leaders to share personal insights about the company, their roles, and how employees contribute to the organization's success.

- **Assign a Peer Mentor:** For the first 90 days, pair each new hire with a peer mentor. Mentors can guide them through informal questions, offer support, and help integrate them into the culture.

- **Build a Resource Library:** Develop a centralized repository for Standard Operating Procedures

(SOPs), tools, and frequently asked questions. Make resources easily accessible online to empower new hires to find answers independently.

- **Conduct Regular Check-Ins:** Schedule supervisor check-ins at key intervals (e.g., end of the first week, 30 days, 60 days, and 90 days). Use these sessions to align on goals, gather feedback, and provide support.

- **Gather Feedback and Iterate:** Survey new hires after their first month to understand what worked well and what needed improvement. Based on feedback and outcomes (e.g., retention rates and engagement levels), continuously refine the onboarding process.

- **Showcase the Bigger Picture:** Incorporate sessions on financial impact, customer success stories, and long-term goals to connect the new hire's role to the organization's success. Create opportunities for cross-department collaboration early to prevent siloed thinking.

- **Leverage Technology for Onboarding:** Use tools like learning management systems (LMS) for interactive training. Implement onboarding software to streamline processes, track completion, and ensure consistency.

- **Celebrate Milestones:** Recognize small wins during the onboarding process, such as completing a significant task or hitting the thirty-day mark. Celebrate with team shout-outs, personalized notes, or small gestures of appreciation.

As we move into the next chapter on "Continuous Employee Development and Career Pathing," we'll explore how to keep that initial momentum going. After the first ninety days, the real challenge becomes keeping employees motivated, growing, and connected to their career goals. The focus shifts from onboarding to providing ongoing support, skill development, and clear opportunities for advancement.

We'll discuss how to create a continuous development plan that strengthens employees' skill sets and offers clear pathways for career progression. By doing so, you'll foster a culture of growth that not only retains top talent but inspires them to become leaders within your organization.

Remember, retaining employees isn't just about keeping them satisfied with where they are—it's about showing them where they could go and how you'll support them in getting there.

Chapter 8

Continuous Employee Development and Career Pathing

"An employee's job is to give his or her best work every day. A manager's job is to give the employee a good reason to come back to work tomorrow."

—LIZ RYAN

As a leader, you've likely heard the phrase, "If you're not growing, you're going." This rings especially true when it comes to employee development. Employees who feel stagnant are more likely to disengage and start looking for opportunities elsewhere. In fact, a LinkedIn survey found that 94 percent of employees would stay at a company longer if it invested in their learning and development.[34] Continuous employee development is an investment in your workforce and a strategic move for business growth and retention.

THE POWER OF LEARNING AND DEVELOPMENT

Implementing formal learning programs can feel daunting for small businesses, especially if resources are limited. However, it doesn't take a giant budget or an entire department to create an impactful development strategy. Sometimes, all it takes is identifying the right opportunities and fostering a culture of learning.

Take a story from a small startup: Initially, the company focused solely on getting products out the door and meeting deadlines. They didn't have time or resources for a formal training program, but as the company grew, they saw employees begin to plateau. Morale dropped, and turnover rates rose. To combat this, the company started implementing low-cost solutions, such as peer mentorships, cross-departmental training, and even an internal book club on leadership and strategy.

These small changes had a huge impact. Employees became more engaged, productivity rose, and the

---

34   AbigailJHess, "LinkedIn: 94% of Employees Say They Would Stay at a Company Longer for This Reason-and It's Not a Raise," CNBC, February 27, 2019, https://www.cnbc.com/2019/02/27/94percent-of-employees-would-stay-at-a-company-for-this-one-reason.html.

company saw a significant reduction in turnover. The moral of the story is that development doesn't have to be complicated or expensive—it just needs to be continuous and intentional.

CAREER PATHING: CREATING CLARITY AND DIRECTION

One of the most powerful tools you can give your employees is a clear career path. When employees understand how they can advance within your company, it gives them something to strive for. Career pathing not only helps you retain your top talent, but it also provides a sense of purpose and motivation for your employees. Gallup research has shown that 87 percent of millennials rate "professional or career growth and development opportunities" as one of the most important aspects of a job.[35]

In one organization I worked with, we realized that many employees didn't see a future for themselves in the company because there was no clear path to advancement. We began by identifying critical roles in each department and defining the skills and experiences required for employees to move up the ladder. We then created personalized development plans for each employee, outlining how they could move into higher roles. By having these conversations, employees felt valued and saw

---

35   Amy Adkins, "What Millennials Want from Work and Life," Gallup.com, October 15, 2024, https://www.gallup.com/workplace/236477/millennials-work-life.aspx.

a future for themselves at the company, which led to increased engagement and a decrease in turnover.

ACTIONABLE STEPS FOR CAREER PATHING

Career pathing doesn't have to be overwhelming. Here are a few actionable steps that can help you create a structured career pathing system in your organization.

- **Identify Critical Roles**: Map out the critical roles in your organization that are essential to your company's growth.

- **Define Required Skills**: For each role, define the necessary skills, experiences, and accomplishments needed to advance.

- **Create Individual Development Plans**: Work with employees to develop personalized plans that outline how they can achieve the required skills and experience for their desired roles.

- **Offer Learning Opportunities**: Provide the resources needed to help employees grow, whether through formal training, online courses, or mentoring.

- **Hold Regular Career Conversations**: Have regular check-ins to discuss progress and adjust their development plans as necessary.

THE ROLE OF MENTORSHIP IN
EMPLOYEE DEVELOPMENT

Mentorship is one of the most powerful—and often underutilized—tools for employee development. It doesn't require a large budget or complex programs, but the benefits are significant. According to the Association for Talent Development (ATD), mentored employees are promoted five times more often than those who are not.[36]

At one small business, I helped implement a mentorship program where senior employees were paired with junior employees for monthly check-ins. These informal meetings gave junior employees the chance to learn from those with more experience, ask questions, and receive guidance on career progression. Over time, this simple program built stronger relationships across the company, fostered a culture of learning, and gave employees a clearer sense of direction in their career path.

Mentorships don't need to be overly formal. They can be as simple as assigning a "buddy" to new hires or setting up monthly check-ins with more senior employees. These connections provide valuable learning experiences for entry or mid-level employees and help senior staff refine their leadership skills, creating a win-win situation.

---

36   "The Power of Mentorship: Statistics Prove Anyone Can Benefit," Asia talent mobility alliance -, October 3, 2023, https://www.asiatma.com/page-18071/13262083.

STATISTICS SUPPORTING CONTINUOUS DEVELOPMENT

The numbers don't lie when it comes to the importance of employee development.

- According to a report by the Work Institute, lack of career development opportunities was the number one reason people left their jobs in 2021, accounting for 22 percent of all voluntary turnover.[37]

- A study by LinkedIn Learning found that employees at companies with internal mobility stay almost twice as long as employees at companies without it.[38]

These stats highlight the tangible impact that continuous learning and career development can have on retention and engagement. Employees want to grow, and if your company isn't providing that opportunity, they'll look for it elsewhere.

LEVERAGING TECHNOLOGY FOR DEVELOPMENT

Technology has made it easier than ever for businesses of all sizes to offer learning and development

---

37   William Mahan, "Career Development: The Top Reason for Leaving a Job: Work Institute," workinstitute.com -, December 22, 2023, https://work-institute.com/blog/career-development-is-the-top-reason-for-leaving-a-job/.

38   "Internal Mobility Playbook: Linkedin Learning," Internal Mobility Playbook | LinkedIn Learning, accessed November 2, 2024, https://learning.linkedin.com/resources/internal-mobility/internal-mobility-playbook.

opportunities. Online courses, webinars, and virtual workshops provide employees with the tools they need to grow without the overhead of traditional classroom-based training.

For instance, platforms like Coursera, LinkedIn Learning, and Udemy offer a wide range of professional development courses, from leadership to technical skills. These platforms are affordable and flexible, allowing employees to learn at their own pace.

Encourage your employees to take advantage of these resources and even offer incentives for completing courses. Whether it's a small bonus, public recognition, or a certificate of completion, rewarding employees for their growth efforts shows them that you're invested in their development.

BUILDING A CULTURE OF CONTINUOUS LEARNING

Creating a culture of learning means fostering an environment where growth and development are prioritized. It's about more than just offering a few training sessions—it's about making learning an integral part of the company culture.

At one company we worked with, we built a culture of learning by incorporating development into the weekly team meetings. Each week, one team member would share something they had learned, whether it was a new skill, best practice, or an industry insight. This not only encouraged employees to seek out learning opportunities actively but also allowed them to share knowledge with the entire team. Over time, this created a culture where learning was celebrated, and employees were motivated to improve continuously.

CAREER DEVELOPMENT AS A RETENTION STRATEGY

One of the most compelling reasons to invest in continuous development is its direct impact on retention. According to Deloitte, companies with strong learning cultures are 92 percent more likely to develop novel products and processes and 52 percent more productive.[39] When employees know that their company is committed to their growth, they are far more likely to stay.

A clear career path, coupled with continuous learning opportunities, fosters loyalty and reduces turnover. Employees who see a future for themselves within the company are more engaged, motivated, and productive. Investing in their development is an investment in your company's success.

---

39   Michael Kriz, "Council Post: Seven Ways to Build a Strong Company Culture," Forbes, August 13, 2024, https://www.forbes.com/councils/forbestechcouncil/2022/12/02/seven-ways-to-build-a-strong-company-culture/.

THE LINK BETWEEN ENGAGEMENT AND DEVELOPMENT

As mentioned earlier, engagement is a critical driver of retention and productivity, and continuous development plays a key role in engagement. Employees who are given opportunities to grow and develop are more engaged in their work. They feel valued and are more likely to invest their time and energy in the company's success.

Engaged employees are also more likely to share their ideas and contribute to innovation. They feel a sense of ownership over their work and are motivated to help the company grow. This is especially important in small businesses, where every employee's contribution can make a significant impact.

CONCLUSION: THE LONG-TERM PAYOFF OF DEVELOPMENT

Continuous development and career pathing are not just strategies—they are commitments to your employees' success and, by extension, your company's success. Investing in your team's growth sends a powerful message: that you value their potential and are willing to support their aspirations. This creates a workplace where employees feel motivated, engaged, and aligned with the company's goals.

As we've seen, development doesn't have to be costly or complex. It can be as simple as fostering mentorship, providing clear career paths, and celebrating a culture of learning. When employees have clarity about their future, access to resources to grow, and a sense of purpose, they become not only better workers but also more vigorous advocates for your organization.

Your role as a leader is to inspire growth, provide direction, and remove barriers to progress. By doing so, you create a workplace where employees choose to stay, thrive, and contribute their best every day.

KEY TAKEAWAYS

- **Growth Prevents Stagnation**: Employees who have opportunities for continuous development are more engaged, motivated, and likely to stay with your company.

- **Career Pathing Builds Loyalty**: Clear career paths give employees a vision for their future within the organization, fostering commitment and reducing turnover.

- **Mentorship Is a Game-Changer**: Even informal mentorship programs can accelerate growth, build relationships, and refine leadership skills across the team.

- **Culture of Learning Is Key**: Incorporate development into everyday practices to make learning a core part of your company's DNA.

- **Technology Expands Opportunities:** Use platforms like LinkedIn Learning and Coursera to provide affordable, flexible learning options for employees.

ACTION STEPS

Here are some actionable steps to help you foster a learning culture in your organization.

- **Set the Tone from the Top**: Leadership must prioritize learning and set an example by participating in development activities themselves.

- **Encourage Knowledge Sharing**: Create opportunities for employees to share what they've learned, whether through presentations, team meetings, or informal lunch-and-learn sessions.

- **Make Learning Accessible**: Offer a variety of learning opportunities, including online courses, webinars, and in-person workshops. Make sure employees have the time and resources they need to participate.

- **Recognize Growth**: Publicly recognize employees who take the initiative to learn and grow. This can be as simple as a shout-out in a meeting or as formal as a monthly award.

- **Tie Development to Career Pathing**: Ensure that learning is tied to career advancement. Make it clear how developing new skills will help employees move forward in their careers.

- **Incorporate Leadership Storytelling**: Have leaders share their personal learning and development journeys during team meetings or town halls. This reinforces the value of growth and shows employees that even leaders continue to learn.

- **Build Peer-Led Learning Communities**: Establish internal groups or committees focused on specific topics, like leadership development or technical skills, where employees can mentor and learn from each other.

- **Provide Structured Learning Time**: Dedicate specific hours each month for employees to focus on skill-building, similar to Google's 20 percent time for personal projects, to ensure learning is prioritized during the workday.[40]

---

40   "Unlocking Creativity: Google's 20% Time Rule for Workplace Success," Eaton Business School, November 18, 2024, https://ebsedu.org/blog/google-tapping-workplace-actualization-20-time-rule.

- **Create Development Budgets**: Allocate a set amount of funding per employee for learning opportunities, such as conferences, certifications, or online courses, to show tangible investment in their growth.

- **Leverage Cross-Functional Projects**: Encourage employees to work on projects outside their usual scope. This builds new skills, fosters collaboration, and gives employees a chance to explore career interests.

- **Integrate Learning into Performance Reviews**: Make discussions about learning and growth a standard part of performance evaluations, encouraging employees to reflect on their development and set future goals.

- **Offer Micro-Learning Options**: Provide quick, accessible learning modules (e.g., five to ten-minute videos or articles) that employees can engage with between tasks, making development more manageable.

- **Celebrate Learning Milestones**: Recognize not just the initiative to learn but also the completion of significant milestones, like finishing a certification or mastering a new skill, with tangible rewards or public acknowledgment.

Incorporating continuous employee development and career pathing into your company's strategy isn't just about keeping employees happy in the short term.

It's about creating a sustainable culture of growth that will drive your business forward for years to come.

By offering clear career paths, encouraging learning, and fostering a culture of development, you're not just building a more skilled workforce—you're building a more engaged, loyal, and motivated team. And that's the key to long-term success.

Chapter 9

Building a Positive Work Environment and Engagement

"There are only three measurements that tell you nearly everything you need to know about your organization's overall performance: employee engagement, customer satisfaction, and cash flow... It goes without saying that no company, small or large, can win over the long run without energized employees who believe in the mission and understand how to achieve it."

—JACK WELCH

A recent LinkedIn poll of 32 business professionals revealed that engagement is the most significant pain point in virtual work.[41] This finding isn't surprising, as engagement is the primary driver of retention, productivity, and performance across all industries. With more companies adopting remote and hybrid models, ensuring employees feel connected and engaged has become both a challenge and an opportunity for leaders who get it right.

In today's evolving workplace, cultivating engagement is no longer optional—it's a fundamental element of business success. Building a workplace where employees feel valued and engaged is critical to retaining top talent and driving long-term growth. Let's explore why engagement matters and how to cultivate it effectively within your organization.

THE ESSENCE OF EMPLOYEE ENGAGEMENT

Employee engagement is more than just a buzzword; it's the driving force behind a thriving organization. It's not just about clocking in and out—it's about employees feeling deeply connected to their work and the company's mission. When employees are engaged, they are not only more productive but also more committed to the organization's success.

According to a 2021 Gallup study, engaged teams show 21 percent greater profitability and are 17

---

41   Petra Mayer & Associates Consulting Inc., "The Top L&D Pain Points of 2022: Overcoming the Challenges of Employee Engagement, Hybrid Work Models, and More," LinkedIn, March 9, 2023, https://www.linkedin.com/pulse/top-ld-pain-points-2022-overcoming-challenges-employee/.

percent more productive.[42] However, only 36 percent of US employees were classified as "engaged" in their work, creating a massive gap between potential and performance.[43] This discrepancy is particularly impactful in small businesses, where each employee plays a critical role in achieving company goals.

Engagement is built in environments where employees feel heard, valued, and supported. It's not about flashy perks or benefits; it's about fostering a culture where employees know their contributions matter. For small business owners, who often juggle multiple roles, engagement may seem abstract, but it can be achieved through consistent, intentional efforts. It starts with listening to employees, creating a sense of belonging, and regularly reinforcing how their roles align with the company's mission.

DEEP DIVE INTO CORE CONCEPTS OF ENGAGEMENT

At the core of engagement is a simple truth: employees need to feel that their work matters. To break it down further, let's explore three fundamental elements of employee engagement.

---

42   Grace He, "Employee Engagement Statistics & Facts," teambuilding.com, November 7, 2022, https://teambuilding.com/blog/employee-engagement-statistics.

43   Jim Harter, "U.S. Employee Engagement Drops for First Year in a Decade," Gallup.com, October 18, 2023, https://www.gallup.com/workplace/388481/employee-engagement-drops-first-year-decade.aspx.

- **Purpose**: Employees who understand how their work ties into the broader company mission 2.5 times are more likely to be engaged.[44] Establishing a clear connection between individual roles and company goals creates a sense of purpose.

- **Feedback**: Regular feedback not only boosts performance but also drives engagement. The Society for Human Resource Management (SHRM) found that companies with frequent feedback practices see a 35 percent increase in engagement compared to those without.[45] Feedback creates a culture of continuous improvement and makes employees feel valued.

- **Recognition**: A University of Massachusetts study revealed that employees who receive regular recognition are three times more likely to be motivated.[46] Recognition can be formal or informal, ranging from a simple "thank you" to a structured rewards program. It signals

---

44   "Qualtrics Announces Top Employee Trends for 2024," Qualtrics, October 25, 2023, https://www.qualtrics.com/news/qualtrics-announces-top-employee-trends-for-2024/.

45   Shweta Agarwal, "SHRM/Globoforce Survey Reveals Human-Centered Approaches in the Workplace Help Organizations Better Recruit and Retain Employees," SHRM/Globoforce Survey Reveals Human-Centered Approaches in the Workplace Help Organizations Better Recruit and Retain Employees | Business Wire, January 24, 2018, https://www.businesswire.com/news/home/20180124005549/en/SHRMGloboforce-Survey-Reveals-Human-Centered-Approaches-in-the-Workplace-Help-Organizations-Better-Recruit-and-Retain-Employees.

46   Andrea Hsu, "Want to Keep Good Workers? Praise Them, a New Study Finds," NPR, September 18, 2024, https://www.npr.org/2024/09/18/nx-s1-5113918/employee-praise-recognition-retention-gallup.

to employees that their contributions are appreciated, driving deeper engagement.

CASE STUDY: SLACK'S EMPLOYEE ENGAGEMENT TRANSFORMATION

Slack, a collaboration software company, encountered significant engagement challenges as it scaled rapidly during the pandemic. Employees—particularly new hires—felt disconnected and isolated. Initial surveys revealed that employees working remotely struggled to find a sense of community and connection to the company's mission.[47]

In response, Slack introduced a comprehensive engagement strategy that included regular virtual events, pulse surveys to gather feedback, and a peer-to-peer recognition platform where employees could earn points and rewards. This platform not only fostered a sense of camaraderie but also allowed employees to feel valued by their peers. Within six months, engagement scores rose by 25 percent, demonstrating the power of intentional, tech-supported engagement efforts. This case highlights that even in virtual settings, engagement can be enhanced through consistent communication and peer acknowledgment.

---

47   Slack, "The Future Is Collaborative: How Communication Platforms Are Shaping the Way We Work," Slack, April 6, 2021, https://slack.com/blog/transformation/future-collaborative-communication-platforms-shaping-way-we-work.

THE ANATOMY OF A HEALTHY WORK CULTURE

Creating a positive and engaging work environment is like sculpting a masterpiece—it takes time, dedication, and consistent effort. As businesses grow, maintaining a cohesive culture becomes more challenging.

I've seen this firsthand at a startup where the initial team of ten to fifteen employees was highly engaged. They were passionate about building the company, and their energy was contagious. They worked closely together, shared goals, and felt a strong sense of ownership over the company's success. However, as the startup grew, communication became more fragmented, and silos started to form. New hires lacked the same connection to leadership and their peers, causing engagement to decline.

This is a common scenario as companies expand. More hands-on leaders may become more distant as they shift to strategic roles, leaving employees feeling disconnected. It's essential to break down silos, promote cross-departmental collaboration, and ensure that communication channels remain open to maintain engagement.

MENTAL HEALTH AND ENGAGEMENT

A positive work environment goes together with mental well-being. Employees are more engaged when they feel supported in managing both work and personal demands. In fact, a 2022 study by Mind Share Partners found that companies prioritizing mental health report 20 percent higher employee satisfaction.[48]

Integrating mental health into engagement strategies doesn't require major changes. Small actions, like offering mental health days, promoting work-life balance, or providing access to counseling resources, can make a significant difference. This shows employees that their well-being is a priority, boosting morale and engagement.

A recent survey I did on LinkedIn showcases how many employees will tell their boss they are "fine" when they are about to have a nervous breakdown. This shows that if an employee doesn't feel safe or comfortable being vulnerable with their boss about their internal or even personal situation that is going on in the background, then it could cause the person's work to be lacking. Disengagement and overall well-being are suffering, while this person could be pushing through to exhaustion and then even get to the point where they just quit because they can't handle the situation any longer.

They feel that they don't have any other way than to leave the company; not recognizing the feeling could lessen with a mental health day, taking a step back,

---

48   "Mind Share Partners' Biennial Mental Health at Work Reports," mindsharepartners, accessed November 2, 2024, https://www.mindsharepartners.org/mentalhealthatworkreports.

or even not feeling alone by talking through it with someone they respect, trust, and feel could validate their concerns.

LEADING WITH PURPOSE AND INTEGRITY

Trust is at the core of engagement. Employees need to trust their leaders and believe that the company's mission aligns with their values. Leaders who act with integrity and communicate transparently build a culture of trust that fosters engagement.

For example, I once worked with a company where the CEO made a point of personally engaging with employees at all levels, from entry-level to management. He knew every employee's name and regularly checked in with team members across departments. This wasn't just a symbolic gesture— employees genuinely felt appreciated, creating a sense of belonging and driving engagement.

Small business owners have a unique advantage in this area: they can maintain closer relationships with their teams. When employees feel connected to their leaders and understand how their work contributes to the company's success, engagement levels rise.

THE POWER OF EMPLOYEE BUY-IN

Getting employees to buy into the company's mission is essential for long-term success. When employees believe in what they're doing, they're more motivated, more productive, and more likely to stay. A Gallup survey found that companies with highly engaged workforces see a 41 percent reduction in absenteeism and a 59 percent decrease in turnover.[49]

Creating buy-in starts with showing employees that their input matters. Regularly ask employees about their goals, career aspirations, and ideas for improving processes. This can be done through one-on-one meetings, team brainstorming sessions, or casual check-ins.

Empowering leaders to make decisions for their team creates a trickle-down effect, empowering leaders to empower employees of their team, too. People don't learn or feel great when they are constantly being told what to do, especially when you hire someone with a certain level of expertise. When you empower people to be in the zone of genius, to make decisions, and to contribute by having a voice in the process, they are bought in. The goal they created was their own, and they were excited to achieve it because they were the ones who came up with it.

---

49   Naz Beheshti, "10 Timely Statistics about the Connection between Employee Engagement and Wellness," Forbes, February 20, 2024, https://www.forbes.com/sites/nazbeheshti/2019/01/16/10-timely-statistics-about-the-connection-between-employee-engagement-and-wellness/.

BUILDING A FEEDBACK LOOP

Feedback is critical to engagement, but it's a two-way street. Employees not only need feedback but also need to feel heard. Establishing a culture of open dialogue—where feedback flows both ways—builds trust and fosters innovation.

Small businesses, with their closer teams, can leverage this dynamic more easily than larger corporations. Regular feedback, casual weekly check-ins, and quarterly reviews ensure that employees feel heard and appreciated. This consistent feedback loop not only drives engagement but also encourages employees to contribute new ideas, enhancing innovation.

TOOLS FOR ENGAGEMENT IN A VIRTUAL WORKPLACE

As remote work becomes more common, engagement strategies need to evolve. The principles of connection, communication, and recognition still apply, but they need to be adapted to virtual settings.

To maintain engagement in remote environments:

- Use communication tools like Slack or Microsoft Teams to keep dialogue flowing.

- Schedule regular virtual check-ins and team meetings to maintain relationships.

- Create virtual team-building activities, such as trivia games, virtual coffee breaks, or themed online events, to foster camaraderie.

A LinkedIn poll revealed that engagement is the biggest challenge in virtual work settings.[50] To address this, leaders must be intentional about creating virtual spaces for interaction, transparency, and consistent recognition.

CONCLUSION: A CONTINUOUS COMMITMENT

Engagement is the lifeblood of a thriving organization, and cultivating it requires intentional effort, clear purpose, and authentic leadership. As we've explored in this chapter, creating an environment where employees feel valued, heard, and connected is not just a nice-to-have—it's a business imperative.

From fostering purpose and feedback loops to prioritizing mental health and leveraging virtual tools, the strategies to enhance engagement are as varied as they are impactful. The stories and data presented here underline a crucial truth: engaged employees drive retention, productivity, and innovation, forming the foundation of long-term success.

Leaders play a pivotal role in shaping this environment. Whether through small acts of recognition, fostering

50   Monica Fike, "Hybrid Workers Most Engaged: Poll," LinkedIn, August 30, 2023, https://www.linkedin.com/news/story/hybrid-workers-most-engaged-poll-5743476/.

open communication, or empowering teams to take ownership, the actions you take today will ripple through your organization's culture and performance.

As you move forward, remember that engagement is not a one-time initiative—it's an ongoing commitment to your people. By building a positive work environment where employees feel deeply connected to their work and your mission, you're not just creating a better workplace; you're making a better business.

Your next step is to take these insights and turn them into action. Start small, measure progress, and stay consistent. When you prioritize engagement, you're not just investing in your employees—you're investing in the future of your organization.

KEY TAKEAWAYS

- **Engagement Is Critical for Success:** Employee engagement directly correlates with retention, productivity, and overall performance. Companies with highly engaged teams experience greater profitability, reduced turnover, and stronger cultures.[51] Prioritizing engagement is essential for sustainable business success.

- **Trust and Communication Build Engagement:** Transparent communication fosters a positive work environment and is fundamental to building trust. When employees trust their leaders and understand the company's goals, they feel more committed and aligned with the organization's mission.

- **Flexibility Enhances Work-Life Balance:** Offering flexible work schedules and remote options not only supports work-life balance but also improves overall engagement. Flexibility is particularly important for virtual teams, helping to reduce burnout and improve job satisfaction.

- **Recognition Is a Powerful Motivator:** Recognizing employees for their efforts and achievements is a major driver of engagement. Consistent acknowledgment boosts morale, fosters loyalty, and encourages continued high performance, creating a positive feedback cycle that benefits the entire organization.

---

51   "From Praise to Profits: The Business Case for Recognition at Work," Workhuman, March 28, 2023, https://www.workhuman.com/resources/reports-guides/from-praise-to-profits-workhuman-gallup-report/?utm_source=bing&utm_medium=cpc&utm_campaign=2160936&utm_content=6nArIXb2TiTa2FBEkHobig&utm_term=2024_wh_sem_nb_awareness_secondary_na_phr_pros-company_engagement&&ms-clkid=b0d78e4789f91caa17c4e96ef2ff5f18&gclid=b0d78e4789f91caa-17c4e96ef2ff5f18&gclsrc=3p.ds.

- **Engagement Must Be Ongoing:** Building and maintaining engagement is an ongoing process that requires consistent communication, regular recognition, and transparent leadership. It's not a one-time initiative but a continuous commitment that shapes a thriving, engaged workplace.

ACTION STEPS

- **Create Clear Lines of Communication:** Establish regular check-ins, team meetings, and feedback loops to ensure employees feel heard and stay informed about company updates and changes. Use tools like Slack, Microsoft Teams, or Zoom for quick and transparent communication.

- **Incorporate Communication Norms:** Promote engagement, such as setting a regular cadence for one-on-ones and team huddles. This will create a predictable rhythm and build trust among team members.

- **Foster a Recognition Culture:** Implement a tiered recognition system that celebrates achievements both big and small, from shout-outs during meetings to formal awards or bonuses. Introduce peer-to-peer recognition programs that empower employees to acknowledge each other's contributions, reinforcing a culture of mutual appreciation and camaraderie.

- **Promote Flexibility:** Offer customizable work arrangements, such as flexible hours, remote work options, or hybrid schedules to foster work-life balance. Be transparent about the flexibility policy so that employees know what's possible and feel supported in managing their personal and professional commitments.

- **Leverage Virtual Engagement Tools:** Use platforms like Slack, Teams, or Zoom to keep remote employees connected through regular check-ins, team-building activities, and virtual social events like coffee breaks or happy hours. Introduce tools like virtual whiteboards or collaboration apps (e.g., Miro, Trello) to facilitate brainstorming and maintain creativity, even in remote environments.

- **Offer Development Opportunities:** Provide learning resources, from online courses to workshops, that are aligned with employee career goals. Make development part of regular performance conversations to highlight pathways for growth. Set up mentorship or buddy programs that allow employees to learn from more experienced team members, fostering engagement and professional growth.

- **Gather Employee Feedback:** Use surveys, suggestion boxes, or informal check-ins to collect regular feedback about engagement, satisfaction, and potential areas for improvement. Be responsive to feedback by taking immediate action on any quick fixes while communicating plans for more complex changes to demonstrate that feedback is valued.

- **Build a Feedback Loop:** Ensure that feedback flows both ways by encouraging open dialogue during one-on-ones, team meetings, and even anonymous surveys. Use the feedback loop to identify trends and potential areas for innovation, making employees feel they are part of shaping the company's future.

- **Align Engagement Efforts with Company Mission:** Regularly reinforce the company's mission, values, and vision during team meetings, updates, and individual check-ins to ensure employees understand how their roles contribute to the larger company goals. Use storytelling to illustrate real-life examples of how employee efforts have driven progress toward the mission, making the connection more tangible.

Building a positive work environment and cultivating engagement is not a one-time effort—it's a continuous commitment to your employees and your company's future. By focusing on transparency, recognition, and purpose-driven communication, small business owners can create a workplace where employees feel valued, motivated, and engaged. This not only improves retention but also drives higher productivity, performance, and a thriving work culture.

Sustainable Success Through Retention: Weaving It All Together

"Train people well enough so they can leave, treat them well enough so they don't want to."

—RICHARD BRANSON

Retention isn't just about longevity; it's about creating an environment where employees feel they are *better off with you than without you.* When leaders focus on enriching the employee experience, retention becomes a natural outcome rather than a forced effort.

Retention benefits employees and is an organizational advantage. It strengthens culture, protects institutional knowledge, and ensures consistency in delivering on the company's mission. Most importantly, it creates an environment where people are empowered to contribute their best ideas, take risks, and grow both personally and professionally.

Retention is about building relationships that evolve over time. It's about recognizing employees as dynamic individuals whose needs, goals, and contributions shift as they grow. Organizations that embrace this evolution become stronger, more innovative, and more adaptable.

Here's what sets retention apart in this context:

- **It Fuels Innovation**: Long-tenured employees often become the innovators who challenge the status quo. They bring historical knowledge and pair it with creative thinking, driving the organization forward.

- **It Builds Resilience**: Retention creates stability and continuity, which is crucial in times of change or uncertainty. Employees who feel secure and supported are better equipped to adapt and problem-solve.

- **It Deepens Trust**: Retention signals to employees that they matter—not just for what they do but for who they are. This trust fosters loyalty and stronger collaboration.

Retention is the culmination of a successful hire-inspire-retain strategy. It starts well before an employee joins the company and continues throughout their journey. Retention is about more than competitive salaries and perks; it's built on clear expectations, structured onboarding, continuous recognition, growth opportunities, and strong leadership. This chapter ties together all three sections—HIRE, INSPIRE, and RETAIN—illustrating how they collectively drive retention and long-term success.

HIRE: LAYING THE FOUNDATION FOR RETENTION

Retention starts at the hiring stage. The hiring process sets the tone for an employee's experience, influencing both their engagement and their decision to stay long-term.

Role Clarity and Job Descriptions

Clear and detailed job descriptions are critical to hiring the right people who will stay. When candidates understand the role, responsibilities, and expectations upfront, they're more likely to align with the position and remain longer. Vague descriptions often lead to mismatches, which can cause frustration and early turnover.

According to a study by Indeed, 63 percent of employees who leave within the first year cite a mismatch between job expectations and the reality of the role.[52] The research shows how crucial it is to set clear expectations from the beginning.

Case Studies: Role Clarity Approach

Netflix emphasizes job clarity to ensure role alignment and reduce turnover.[53] Unlike typical job descriptions that focus only on tasks, Netflix outlines expected outcomes, company culture, and metrics for success. This approach attracts candidates who understand not only what the job entails but also how their work impacts the organization's mission from day one. The result? Netflix has one of the lowest turnover rates in the industry, demonstrating how clear role expectations contribute to higher retention.

Similarly, HubSpot takes job clarity seriously.[54] The company doesn't just describe the job; it specifies expected outcomes, cultural fit, and the skills needed to excel. By providing this detailed information upfront, HubSpot has reduced new hire turnover by 35 percent within the first year. When candidates

---

52   Indeed Editorial Team, "16 Reasons Why Employees Choose to Leave Their Jobs | Indeed.Com," Indeed: Career Guide, September 9, 2024, https://www.indeed.com/career-advice/career-development/reasons-employees-leave.

53   Untitled Leader, "Leading the Netflix Way: Unveiling Key Lessons for Success in Today's Dynamic Landscape," Untitled Leader, July 22, 2024, https://www.untitledleader.com/lessons-in-leadership/leading-the-netflix-way-unveiling-key-lessons-for-success-in-todays-dynamic-landscape/.

54   Kevin Kruse, "How Hubspot Sustains a Customer-Centric Culture across 7K Hybrid Employees," Forbes, September 6, 2023, https://www.forbes.com/sites/kevinkruse/2023/09/05/how-hubspot-sustains-a-customer-centric-culture-across-7k-hybrid-employees/.

know exactly what to expect, they're less likely to experience "buyer's remorse" after joining, which sets a strong foundation for long-term retention.

Clear, detailed job descriptions are more than just hiring tools—they are powerful retention strategies. By setting realistic expectations and aligning candidates with the company's culture and mission, organizations can reduce early turnover and build a more committed workforce.

The Interview Process: Assessing for Fit and Longevity

The interview process is the next step in building a foundation for retention. As detailed in Chapter 3, using a structured approach that includes behavioral, competency-based, and values-based questions can help identify candidates who align with the organization's values and culture.

- **Resilience-Focused Interviewing Impact on Retention:** Studies show that assessing resilience during the interview process can positively affect retention rates. Research indicates that resilience-focused training programs and hiring processes lead to improved employee well-being and performance, contributing to higher engagement and longer retention. One study found that employees with solid resilience skills were more likely to exhibit better adaptability and lower turnover rates, as they could handle job stressors more effectively .[55] While exact percentage reductions in turnover can vary across organizations, the emphasis on resilience has been consistently linked to higher retention.

- **Google's Holistic Interviewing and Retention:** Google's structured interviewing approach—using behavioral and cultural fit assessments coupled with a hiring committee—is designed to reduce bias and enhance candidate alignment with company values.[56] This comprehensive process has been linked to better retention outcomes. Google's focus on holistic assessments, which includes resilience and adaptability, has been noted for reducing overall turnover compared to industry averages, particularly among tech roles where fit and adaptability are crucial.

- **Integrating the Candidate Experience Into Retention:** Retention begins with a positive candidate experience. As highlighted in Chapters 1 and 2, candidates who feel valued during the hiring process are more likely to remain engaged after being hired. Simple gestures like

55   Kristin L. Cullen et al., "Employees' Adaptability and Perceptions of Change-Related Uncertainty: Implications for Perceived Organizational Support, Job Satisfaction, and Performance - Journal of Business and Psychology," SpringerLink, June 8, 2013, https://link.springer.com/article/10.1007/s10869-013-9312-y.
56   "Google Interview Process: A Comprehensive Insider's Guide," Hello Interview, accessed December 13, 2024, https://www.hellointerview.com/blog/google-interview-process.

clear communication, timely feedback, and personalized touchpoints can make candidates feel more connected to the company even before they start. According to LinkedIn, 83 percent of candidates say a negative interview experience can change their opinion about a role they initially liked.[57] Conversely, a positive interview experience can increase acceptance rates by 40 percent.

INSPIRE: CREATING A CULTURE OF ENGAGEMENT AND GROWTH

Once employees are hired, the focus shifts to inspiring them to grow and remain engaged. As discussed in Chapters 4 through 6, recognition, feedback, and career development are crucial elements in retaining employees and fostering a thriving culture.

The Power of Recognition

Recognition isn't just a motivational tool; it's a key driver of retention. Employees who feel appreciated are more likely to stay committed to their roles. The 2021 Gallup Workplace Report states that employees who receive regular recognition are four times more

---

57   Andrew Fennell, "Candidate Experience Statistics 2024: Regularly Updated," StandOut CV | Create a winning CV in minutes with our simple CV builder, August 5, 2024, https://standout-cv.com/candidate-experience-statistics.

likely to stay with their employer than those who do not.[58]

Case Study: Adobe's Continuous Recognition Approach

Adobe revamped its performance review system by introducing "check-ins," where managers have regular, informal conversations with employees about achievements, areas for improvement, and alignment with company values. This continuous recognition approach replaced the annual review process, leading to a 30 percent increase in employee engagement and a reduction in turnover by 25 percent.[59] Adobe's employees report feeling more valued, which directly impacts their decision to stay long-term.

Feedback: Creating a Culture of Continuous Improvement

Feedback must be a two-way street to be effective. It's not just about managers giving feedback; it's about employees having the opportunity to share their thoughts as well. According to SHRM, 68 percent of employees who receive consistent feedback feel more engaged.[60]

58   Ryan Pendell, "7 Gallup Workplace Insights: What We Learned in 2021," Gallup.com, January 1, 2022, https://www.gallup.com/workplace/358346/gallup-workplace-insights-learned-2021.aspx.
59   Brian Miller, "How We Inspire Great Performance at Adobe," Adobe Blog, May 9, 2022, https://blog.adobe.com/en/publish/2022/05/09/how-we-inspire-great-performance-at-adobe.
60   Think Learning and Matt Mundey, "13 Essential Employee Feedback Statistics," Think Learning, November 22, 2023, https://www.think-learning.com/employee-engagement/employee-feedback-statistics/.

- **Example:** At a large healthcare organization, feedback sessions were integrated into weekly meetings. These feedback loops were not only used for performance but also for understanding how employees felt about their roles and career progression. This practice led to a 17 percent increase in employee retention over one year, as employees felt their voices were heard and valued.

Career Development: Paving the Way for Retention

Employees are more likely to stay when they see a path for growth. LinkedIn's 2021 Workplace Learning Report revealed that 94 percent of employees would stay longer at a company that invests in their development.[61] Creating personalized growth plans, offering skill-building workshops, and providing opportunities for mentorship can significantly enhance retention.

Case Study: Amazon's Career Development Pathways

Amazon's career development programs include both technical training and management tracks, allowing employees to choose paths that align with their interests and strengths. This approach provides clear career pathways and opportunities for growth, reducing turnover by 35 percent among entry-level

---

61   "2021 Workplace Learning Report: Linkedin Learning," 2021 Workplace Learning Report | LinkedIn Learning, accessed November 4, 2024, https://learning.linkedin.com/resources/workplace-learning-report-2021.

employees.[62] Employees who see a future at the company are more likely to remain engaged and committed.

Investing in career development is one of the most effective retention strategies. Employees who feel supported in their growth are more likely to stay loyal to the company.

RETAIN: CULTIVATING A CULTURE THAT ENCOURAGES LONGEVITY

The final step is to retain employees by maintaining engagement, promoting work-life balance, and building a strong sense of community.

The Role of Engagement in Retention

Engagement is not just a phase—it's an ongoing process that requires consistent attention. Engaged employees are more productive, have higher job satisfaction, and are significantly less likely to leave. According to Gallup, companies with high employee

---

62   Amazon Staff, "A New Workplace Study Highlights the Importance of Amazon's Programs for Career Growth and Skills Development," About Amazon, October 31, 2022, https://www.aboutamazon.com/news/work-place/a-new-workplace-study-highlights-the-importance-of-amazons-career-op-portunity-and-skills-development-programs.

engagement see a 59 percent lower turnover rate than those with low engagement.[63]

Story Spotlight: Engagement Strategies at Buffer

Buffer, known for its remote-first culture, emphasizes transparency, well-being, and inclusion.[64] Buffer openly shares company financials, decision-making processes, and employee salaries, which fosters trust and engagement. The company also offers unlimited paid time off and mental health resources, creating a holistic approach to employee well-being. Buffer has maintained a 92 percent retention rate over three years, even during shifts to remote work, proving that a transparent and supportive culture drives retention.

Promoting Work-life Balance

Supporting employees' lives outside of work is critical for retention. Offering flexible schedules, remote work options, and generous leave policies demonstrates a company's commitment to employee well-being.

---

63   "From Praise to Profits: The Business Case for Recognition at Work," Workhuman, September 5, 2024, https://www.workhuman.com/resources/reports-guides/from-praise-to-profits-workhuman-gallup-report/?utm_source=bing&utm_medium=cpc&utm_campaign=2160936&utm_content=6nArIXb2TiTa2FBEkHobig&utm_term=2024_wh_sem_nb_awareness_secondary_na_phr_pros-company_engagement&&msclkid=4c-85348cb43d173ed96253aa1d1afda4&gclid=4c85348cb43d173ed96253aa1d1afda4&gclsrc=3p.ds.

64   "State of Remote Work 2018," Buffer, accessed November 4, 2024, https://buffer.com/state-of-remote-work/2018.

- **Example:** HubSpot encourages employees to take "unplugged weeks" where they fully disconnect from work.[65] This policy has reduced burnout and increased retention rates by 20 percent over two years. Employees return feeling refreshed, appreciated, and motivated to continue contributing.

Promoting work-life balance not only enhances employee satisfaction but also leads to higher retention rates.

The Financial Impact of Turnover

Turnover is expensive. According to the Society for Human Resource Management (SHRM), replacing an employee can cost up to two times their annual salary, factoring in recruitment, onboarding, training, and lost productivity.[66] Beyond financial costs, turnover also disrupts team dynamics, client relationships, and overall morale.

---

65   HubSpot, "Hybrid at HubSpot," HubSpot, accessed November 4, 2024, https://www.hubspot.com/hybrid?irclickid=ypjQpP0CsxyKT-1C3YfXw1ywrUkCW-EVexV5Qw00&irgwc=1&mpid=2003851&utm_id=am2003851&utm_medium=am&utm_source=am2003851&utm_campaign=amcid_ypjQpP0CsxyKT1C3YfXw1ywrUkCW-EVexV5Qw00_irpid_2003851.

66   "Employee Retention: What Employee Turnover Really Costs Your Company," MGR Workforce, February 22, 2023, https://mgrworkforce.com/employers/employee-retention-costs/.

Case Study: Zappos' Unique Retention Strategy

Zappos offers new hires $2,000 to leave after their first week if they don't feel like a good fit.[67] This investment ensures that only those who are genuinely committed stay, contributing to Zappos' high retention rates. Employees who choose to stay are typically more engaged, satisfied, and aligned with the company's culture.

Prioritizing cultural fit from the beginning leads to stronger retention and a more cohesive team.

CONCLUSION: SUSTAINABLE SUCCESS THROUGH RETENTION

Retention is the ultimate measure of a successful hire-inspire-retain strategy. It reflects how effectively an organization aligns its mission, culture, and people to create a thriving workplace. As we've explored in this chapter, retention is not a standalone initiative—it is the product of every step along the employee journey, from hiring with clarity to inspiring engagement and fostering long-term loyalty.

Bringing it all together, we see that retention is built on a foundation of intentional actions:

---

67   Vsadmin, "Zappos Raises Their Quitting Bonuses?," Visibility Software, November 6, 2022, https://visibilitysoftware.com/zappos-raises-their-quitting-bonuses/.

- **Clear job descriptions and structured interviews** ensure the right candidates join the team.

- **Recognition, feedback, and career development** keep employees inspired and engaged.

- **Work-life balance and strong leadership** cultivate a culture where employees feel valued and motivated to stay.

The insights and examples throughout this book illustrate one powerful truth: sustainable success is achieved when organizations prioritize their people. Engaged and fulfilled employees don't just stay—they contribute to innovation, productivity, and long-term growth.

As you close this book, reflect on how you can apply these strategies to your organization. Retention isn't about perfection; it's about consistent progress and a genuine commitment to your team. By focusing on hiring right, inspiring consistently, and fostering an environment where employees want to stay, you're not just retaining talent—you're building a legacy of success.

Your next chapter starts now. Take what you've learned, adapt it to your unique context, and continue weaving together a workplace where people thrive and success follows naturally.

KEY TAKEAWAYS

- **Retention Starts Early**: Clarity in hiring and a positive candidate experience lay the groundwork for long-term retention.

- **Onboarding Is Critical**: Effective onboarding increases retention and helps employees feel valued from the start.

- **Recognition Drives Retention**: Consistent recognition is crucial for employee satisfaction and long-term loyalty.

- **Feedback Is Essential**: Regular feedback keeps employees aligned with goals and committed to the company.

- **Career Growth Keeps Employees**: Investing in development leads to higher retention.

- **Engagement Reduces Turnover**: Engaged employees are less likely to leave, leading to a stronger company culture.

- **Work-Life Balance Matters**: Supporting employees' well-being drives long-term retention.

ACTION STEPS

- **Evaluate Job Descriptions**: Ensure they are clear, detailed, and aligned with company culture to set the foundation for retention.

- **Strengthen the Interview Process**: Use structured questions that assess both skills and cultural fit to select candidates who are likely to stay long-term.

- **Revamp Onboarding**: Implement a structured onboarding process that helps new hires feel connected and valued from day one.

- **Build a Recognition Program**: Create formal and informal systems for consistent acknowledgment of employee achievements.

- **Promote Career Development**: Offer clear growth paths, training opportunities, and mentorship programs to keep employees engaged.

- **Encourage Continuous Feedback**: Establish a culture where feedback is frequent, two-way, and aligned with growth.

- **Promote Work-life Balance**: Offer flexible work options and well-being resources to support employee satisfaction and retention.

Retention is about more than keeping employees—it's about creating a work environment where they want to stay. It requires strategic investment at every stage of the employee lifecycle, from hiring to onboarding and from recognition to career development. By focusing on transparency, consistent engagement, and growth, businesses can achieve sustainable success through retention.

When employees thrive, so does the business. Retention drives productivity, improves performance, and fosters a cohesive culture that ultimately leads to long-term success.

Moving Forward

As I bring this book to a close, I want to take a moment to thank you for coming along on this journey. Writing this has been both a reflection of my own experiences and a vision for what's possible when we focus on people-first strategies. This book has equipped you with actionable insights, inspired new ideas, and perhaps even challenged you to see talent management in a new light.

I hope this glimpse into my experiences inspires you to build workplaces where people not only work but thrive. Whether you're leading a small business, managing a team, or preparing for your next big step, remember that success starts with your people.

I would be incredibly happy if this book helps you create an environment where employees feel valued, connected, and engaged—where hiring is intentional, inspiration is a daily practice, and retention becomes a natural outcome.

To continue your journey, I invite you to stay connected. Follow me on LinkedIn: https://www.

<u>linkedin.com/in/angelatait/</u> where I share exclusive insights, strategies, and tools to help you hire, inspire, and retain top talent. You can also access my **https://bit.ly/freejobdescription** which includes a job description template, checklists, and resources to put the concepts from this book into action. Feel free to book a call and learn more about my services to work together: <u>https://bit.ly/hrsubscription</u>.

I'd love to hear from you! Whether you've implemented an idea, faced a challenge, or simply want to share your experience, feel free to reach out. Together, we can keep the conversation going and continue building better workplaces for everyone.

Finally, I leave you with this: creating a people-first culture isn't always easy, but it's always worth it. Keep investing in your team, trusting in the process, and believing in the power of collaboration. The future of work is in your hands—make it a place where people are inspired to do their best and be their best.

Here's to your continued success and the lasting impact you'll create!

www.AngelaTait.com

Thank You for Reading

The Human Capital Playbook!

I really appreciate your feedback and

I love hearing what you have to say.

I need your input to make the next version of this

book and my future books better.

Please take two minutes now to
leave a helpful review on

Amazon letting me know what
you thought of the book:

www.AngelaTait.com

Thanks so much!

-Angela Tait

Acknowledgments

This book would not have been possible without the incredible support, guidance, and encouragement I've received along the way.

To my parents, thank you for instilling in me the values of hard work, resilience, and kindness. Your belief in me has been a constant source of strength and inspiration.

To Brett, my amazing book coach, your guidance helped bring my vision to life. Thank you for your patience and insights and for pushing me to dig deeper with every chapter.

To my clients, thank you for trusting me with your business and for giving me the opportunity to learn, grow, and create alongside you. Your challenges, successes, and feedback shaped the foundation of this book.

To Ryan, my husband and my partner in everything—thank you for your unwavering support, patience, and love. You are my sounding board, my rock, and my greatest source of encouragement. Your belief in me, even during the moments I doubted myself, has made all the difference. To my kids, Henry and Oliver, who remind me every day how special it is to be loved by you—your belief in me, your childlike spirit, and your playfulness bring so much joy and perspective to my life. You inspire me to approach each day with wonder, creativity, and an open heart.

To Jeannie, my talented editor, thank you for polishing my words and ensuring this book shines. Your attention to detail and creative insights were invaluable.

To my previous employers, thank you for the experiences, lessons, and opportunities that shaped my career and perspective. Each step along the way has been part of the journey leading here.

To my friends and family, your support, feedback, and encouragement have been my lifeline. Thank you for cheering me on, lending your perspectives, and being my community.

This book is as much yours as it is mine. Thank you for walking alongside me on this path and for believing in the vision of creating workplaces that inspire, empower, and retain incredible talent. I am deeply grateful.

About the Author

Angela Tait is the founder of Tait Consulting, LLC, and a dedicated people operations strategist passionate about helping organizations build strong, engaged teams. Holding a Society of Human Resource Certified Professional (SHRM-CP) certification and a Master's in Organization Development (MSOD) from Pepperdine Graziadio Business School, Angela brings over a decade of corporate experience across diverse industries to her work.

Angela empowers leaders to save time, retain top talent, and enhance profitability. Her insights and expertise have been featured in USNews, FastCompany, CNN, Business.Com, SHRM, ABC, NBC, and more, making her a trusted voice in talent management and organizational strategy.

A Southern California native, Angela now resides in Phoenix, Arizona, with her husband and two boys. When she's not helping leaders transform their businesses, she enjoys time at the beach, traveling to other countries, savoring great food, and embracing her love for adventure.

www.ingramcontent.com/pod-product-compliance
Lightning Source LLC
Chambersburg PA
CBHW070927210326
41520CB00021B/6828